William Edward Cousins

Madagascar of To-Day

A sketch of the island, with chapters on its past history and present prospects

William Edward Cousins

Madagascar of To-Day
A sketch of the island, with chapters on its past history and present prospects

ISBN/EAN: 9783337316877

Printed in Europe, USA, Canada, Australia, Japan

Cover: Foto ©ninafisch / pixelio.de

More available books at **www.hansebooks.com**

MADAGASCAR OF TO-DAY.

A Sketch of the Island,

WITH CHAPTERS ON ITS PAST HISTORY
AND PRESENT PROSPECTS.

BY THE

REV. W. E. COUSINS,

Missionary of the London Missionary Society since 1862.

WITH A MAP.

FLEMING H. REVELL COMPANY,
NEW YORK   CHICAGO
112, FIFTH AVENUE.   148 & 150, MADISON ST.
The Religious Tract Society, London.
1895.

LONDON:
PRINTED BY WILLIAM CLOWES AND SONS, LIMITED,
STAMFORD STREET AND CHARING CROSS.

INTRODUCTION.

FROM the time when Marco Polo, the great Venetian traveller, wrote his half-mythical account of Madagascar to this year of grace 1895, in which we scan our daily paper to see how France is faring in her endeavour to persuade the Hova Government to accept a French protectorate, is a far cry. Six centuries lie between these two points.

The Madagascar of Marco Polo was a *terra incognita*, known only by vague rumour. The Madagascar of to-day is an island well known to many Europeans, and has been carefully studied and explored, especially by Frenchmen. Witness, for example, the magnificent work of M. Grandidier, which is likely to fill a score or so of folio volumes, and is a marvel of full and exact knowledge of almost everything relating to the island.

Madagascar seems likely to hold a large place in the thoughts of the British public during the coming years; and the aim of this modest volume is to set forth in brief the main facts as to the country and its people and history, and so enable the reader to form a sound opinion as to the present situation, and to read with intelligence the news that will probably be reaching us from month to month.

INTRODUCTION.

When on my return to England a few months ago I was asked to write a book on Madagascar, my answer was that there seemed to be too many already. I am assured, however, by those who know, that a small book, giving in concise form such information as is needed by ordinary intelligent readers to enable them better to understand how the present crisis has arisen, and what is the actual condition of the country, will be welcomed by many. I have therefore done my best to supply this desideratum. The book has been written *currente calamo*, but the information it contains will, I believe, be found reliable. It is but an outline, and those who desire fuller information may find it in abundance in the works of Ellis, Sibree, Oliver, Grandidier, or in the seventeen published numbers of the Antananarivo Annual.

At the risk of being considered egotistic, I have occasionally preferred to use the first personal pronoun, as I think, when narrating events that have fallen under my personal observation, my doing so adds life and interest to the story.

W. E. COUSINS.

CONTENTS.

	PAGE
CHAPTER I.	
THE LAND	11
CHAPTER II.	
ANTANANARIVO, THE CAPITAL . .	22
CHAPTER III.	
THE PEOPLE	36
CHAPTER IV.	
THE GOVERNMENT	48
CHAPTER V.	
THE GROWTH OF THE HOVA POWER, WITH SOME ACCOUNT OF RECENT SOVEREIGNS . . .	61
CHAPTER VI.	
THE ANCIENT RELIGION OF THE HOVA. . .	75
CHAPTER VII.	
THE INTRODUCTION OF CHRISTIANITY . . .	81

CHAPTER VIII.

THE QUARTER OF A CENTURY WHEN 'THE LAND WAS DARK' 91

CHAPTER IX.

THE RENEWAL OF MISSIONARY WORK . . . 100

CHAPTER X.

BIBLE TRANSLATION 115

CHAPTER XI.

THE PRESENT STATE OF CHRISTIANITY IN THE ISLAND 125

CHAPTER XII.

THE POLITICAL SITUATION 146

LIST OF ILLUSTRATIONS.

Ranavalomanjàka III., Queen of Madagascar	*Frontispiece*	
Map of Madagascar	,,	10
View of the Mangòro . . .	*page*	17
Antananarivo from the North . . .	,,	23
Rainilaiarivòny, Prime Minister of Madagascar	,,	51
Radàma I..	,,	65
David Jones	,,	82
David Griffiths	,,	83
Rainandrìamampàndry, Governor of Tamatave	,,	105
Malagasy Church—Old Style . . .	,,	112
Ambatonakànga Memorial Church . .	,,	129
The London Missionary Society's College .	,,	133
The New Hospital at Isoàvinandriàna . .	,,	137
The Committee of an Antananarivo Y. P. S. C. E.	,,	141

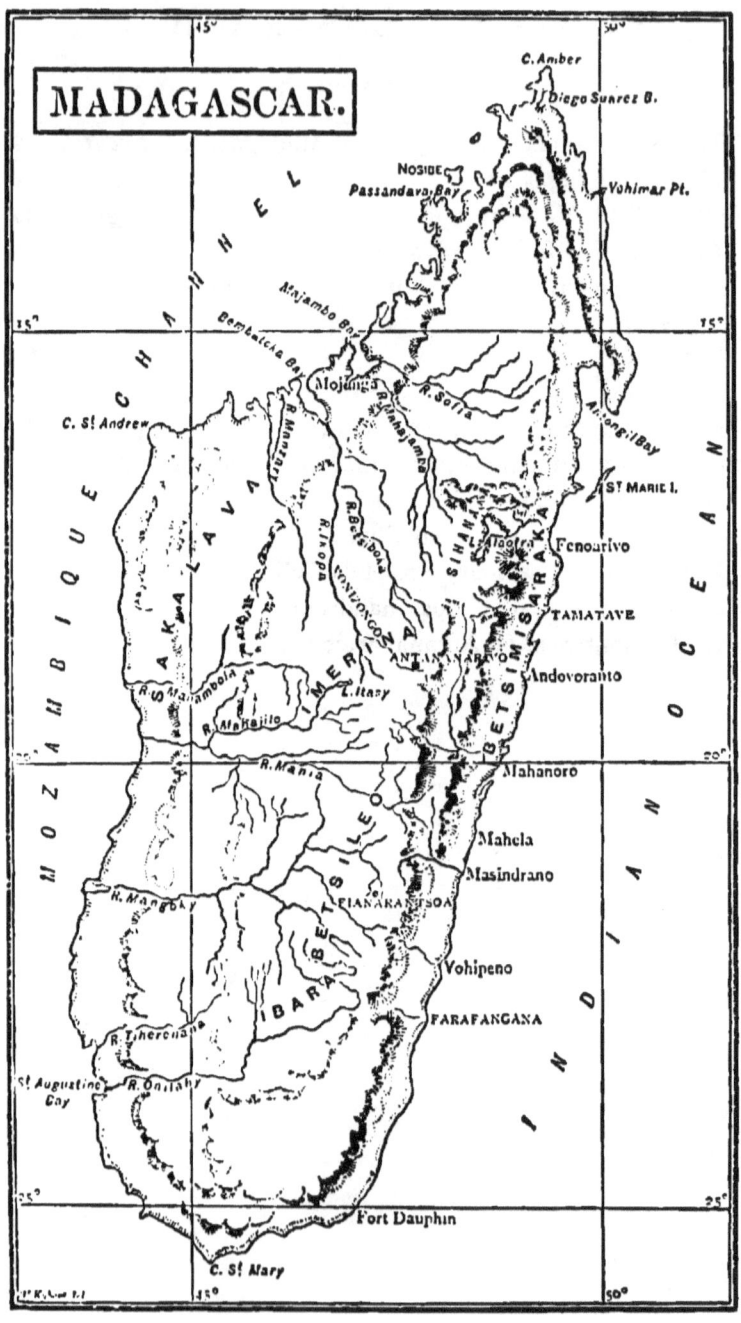

MADAGASCAR OF TO-DAY.

CHAPTER I.

THE LAND.

THE origin of the name Madagascar is still a puzzle. It does not seem to be a native name, and cannot, like the ordinary place names of the country, be explained from the language as we know it to-day. By the natives their island was called *Izao rehètra izao* (The Universe), or *Ny anivon' ny rìaka* (What is in the midst of the floods). Madagascar seems to have been a name imposed from without, and not improbably arose from Marco Polo's confounding it with Magadoxo, on the adjoining coast of Africa, as his use of the word in the thirteenth century is the earliest known; though his description of the island as containing camels and giraffes, panthers and lions, shows that he knew little about it. The spelling of the name in the early authorities is very uncertain, and the following are only some of the variants: Madeigascar, Madeigascat, Madagastar, Magastar.

Canon Isaac Taylor suggests an explanation of the name that indicates a mixed origin, *gosse* being an old Swahili word for man, and *malay* meaning mountains; the *ar* he takes to be a Malay suffix, like the final syllable in Zanzibar, Nicobar. The meaning would therefore be, 'The country of the hill men'; or, if the *d* should be insisted on, 'The country of the *Madai*,' Madai being regarded as an African tribe.

The earliest geographical document in which the island of Madagascar is found indicated is said by M. Grandidier to be the globe of Martin Behain (1492).

A very complete atlas of old maps has been published by M. Grandidier; and it is extremely interesting to notice how the ideas of geographers became gradually more and more correct, until we reach the exact workmanship of Captain W. F. W. Owen in 1825. The outlines of the island were correctly laid down in his chart, but many hands have been at work since, filling up the outlines and showing the physical features and political divisions of the interior.

The island, now so well known to us, lies near the eastern coast of Africa, separated from it by the Mozambique Channel, and distant about 240 miles from the nearest point of the mainland. It extends from 12° 2' to 25° 18' south latitude, and measures nearly 1000 miles in length; and the breadth from east to west is in some parts as much as 350 miles, though the average breadth is about 250 miles. It is estimated to contain about 230,000 square miles.

Madagascar is often conveniently spoken of as the Great African Island, very much, one would think, on the *lucus a non lucendo* principle. It is, geographically speaking, an African island, as it lies near to the great continent, and may, indeed, in very remote ages have been part of it. But its people are not on the whole an African people; and much in its flora and fauna indicates a very long separation from the neighbouring continent. Particularly noticeable is the fact that Madagascar has no lions, elephants, deer, or antelopes, which are abundant in Africa.

Other names have been given to the island by writers and travellers, such as 'The Great Britain of Africa,' which now seems unlikely to become a fact. French writers, with apparently more of the prophetic spirit, rejoice in naming it 'Oriental France,' and recently a French statesman has spoken of it as 'Southern Australia.' How far the prophetic dreams embodied in these names will be realised history will declare.

The physical features of Madagascar may be best understood if we bear in mind that in the interior is an elevated granitic region (using granitic in a popular sense) three thousand to five thousand feet above the level of the sea, and stretching from 13° to 24° south latitude—that is, a distance of more than 700 miles, with an average breadth of about 150. This central region is estimated to contain 100,000 square miles, and this is, on the whole, bare and uninteresting; but some of the lower parts of the country are beautiful and very productive.

Perhaps the best way to give a general idea of the various sections of the country will be to describe them as they appear to a traveller from the coast to the capital, as in taking this journey the main characteristics of the country pass one by one under his observation.

We start, then, from Tamatave, now an important seaport with a large population composed mainly of Mauritians and Bourbonnais, Indians, Chinamen, with a small sprinkling of French, English, American, and German residents. The Malagasy now, for the most part, live on the outskirts of the town.

The journey from Tamatave to Andovorànto (a distance of about sixty miles) lies along the coast, sometimes on the beach itself, but always within a short distance of the ceaseless roar of the Indian Ocean. Much of the country has a beautiful park-like appearance. The turf is soft and velvety, and groups of tropical trees, such as the sago palm, the screw pine (*pandanus*), and the strychnos, are very abundant. What would not an American millionaire give, could he transfer some of this lovely park to his own estate? The admirer of orchids would be delighted to see the rich luxuriance of the *angræcum superbum*, with its wealth of white shell-like blossoms. These grow, for the most part, upon old and decaying trees, and sometimes twelve or fifteen distinct plants, each full of waxen flowers, may be seen growing on a single trunk. Ferns and climbing plants ornament the larger trees in rich abundance.

Almost continuous lagoons lie to the traveller's right hand on this part of the journey, giving variety and beauty to the landscape. These lagoons stretch for a distance of 300 miles along the eastern coast; and Radàma I. began to construct connecting canals, so as to form a continuous water-way. No further work in this direction has been undertaken since his death; but doubtless at some future time a more enterprising and energetic government than the present will utilise this great natural provision, and thus promote the interests of commerce and civilisation. Much of the cloth carried by bearers to the capital is even now carried as far as possible by canoes along these lagoons.

On reaching Andovorànto, the route to Antananarivo turns suddenly inland; and the first stage of the journey is a canoe ride of twelve or fifteen miles up the broad river Ihàroka to the town of Maròmby. The banks of the river are dotted with the small villages of the Betsimisàraka tribe, and the patches of ground that are cultivated show that the soil is rich, and that under proper cultivation it might produce tenfold what is now obtained.

On leaving Maròmby, the traveller still proceeds westwards through a country that appears one mass of hills. These become higher as he advances inland. Some parts of the country are very beautiful. About Ranomafàna, for instance, one is reminded of our own hilly Devonshire; but the vegetation is different, and in this part of the country almost the only trees to be seen are the *raofia* palm (from which the *raffia* fibre is obtained), the traveller's tree, with its fan-like spreading leaves, and the bamboo, which with its bright green feathery leaves and its wondrously graceful curves gives an indescribable charm to the landscape.

Still reaching higher ground as he proceeds westwards, the traveller comes in two or three days to the eastern border of the great forest, which forms a continuous belt round most of the island midway between the seaboard and the central plateau. Here the real difficulties of the journey begin, and the steep and rough tracks that have to be climbed or descended are such as may well fill the least nervous with some amount of apprehension. But the experienced and sure-footed bearers cheerily pursue their way, now wading knee-deep through a marshy valley, now following the bed of some mountain stream, and anon facing bravely one of those steep ascents, or cautiously descending into the next valley, the descent being often a more serious undertaking than the climb upwards. Trees have been felled, and a way has been cleared through this forest; but often trees fall across the track and obstruct the way, and yet no one thinks it his duty to remove them. After about a day and a half of this kind of travelling the western edge of the great forest is reached, and the traveller finds himself in the large garrison town of Mòramànga, where a Hova governor resides. Before him lies the plain of Ankay, twelve or fifteen miles broad, through which the river Mangòro finds its way to the sea south of Mahanòro. Before him in the distance is the steep hill called Ifòdy, and further west is the lofty Angàvo. At this latter point the ascent is very steep, and an advancing army might meet with serious check.

West of Angàvo the road winds among the hills, and two or three times descends into deep and richly-wooded valleys. But after a few miles of this kind of travelling Ankèramadìnika is reached,

C

and before the expectant traveller now lie spread open the bare and almost treeless hills and moors of Imèrina.

Imèrina, strictly so called, extends for about sixty or eighty miles east and west, and for about eighty or a hundred miles north and south; but its limits are not very strictly defined. It is the home of the Hova tribe, and barren and bleak as it is, possesses a beauty of its own. The landscape consists of one vast confusion of bare hills; while huge bosses of granite or gneiss jut out of them in all directions. Their sides also are deeply scarred and cut into gullies and ravines by the tropical rains, exposing the deep-red soil that prevails throughout the country. The grass is green for a few weeks only during the spring, but for most of the year it is scanty and brown.

The first view of this part of the country, especially to one who has just come from the well-wooded regions to the eastward, is generally disappointing. On closer acquaintance, however, the country is found to have some redeeming qualities. Some of the hill-tops are crowned with groups of ancient trees, chiefly of the *ficus* order; little villages composed of houses built of the deep red soil, and looking in the distance like red brick, are perched here and there in all directions; and all the available valleys are carefully cultivated for rice.

Our first feeling as we gaze on this province is: 'Can this barren-looking country produce food enough to feed its million of inhabitants?' But as we proceed westward it becomes a little more open, until we observe that near Antananarivo, and especially to the west of it, there are extensive rice grounds. The great valley of Betsimitàtatra, for instance, once a broad lake, stretches for many miles, and winds in and out among the hills. The sight of this far-spreading valley when the rice crop is well advanced is one not easily forgotten, and it does much to reassure the sceptical as to the food-producing power of Imèrina. His faith will be further confirmed by a visit to the great weekly market described in Chapter II., and he will leave the busy scene with a firm belief in the capacity of the country to supply in rich profusion all the ordinary wants of the people. Bad seasons are rare in the country, and scarcity and famine are hardly known.

The following beautiful little piece of word-painting tells us how the country near Antananarivo appeared to a man of such world-wide experience as the late and much-lamented Cameron, the war-correspondent of the *Standard* newspaper:—

'Antananarivo itself was in sight; and we could plainly see the glass windows of the palace glistening in the morning sun on the top of the long hill on which the city was built. It was Sunday, and the people were clustering along the footpaths on their way to church, or sitting in the grass outside waiting for the service to begin, as they do in villages at home. The women, who appeared to be in the majority, wore white cotton gowns, often neatly embroidered, and white, or black and white, striped lambas thrown gracefully over their shoulders. The men were clad also in cotton—white cotton pantaloons, cotton lambas, and straw hats with large black silk band. In the morning sun the play of colours over the landscape was lovely. The dark green hills, studded with the brilliant red brick houses of the inhabitants, whose white garments dotted the lanes and footpaths, contrasted with the brighter emerald of the rice fields in the hollows. The soil everywhere is deep red, almost magenta, in colour, and where the roads or pathways cross the hills, they shine out as if so many paint-brushes had streaked the country in broad red stripes. Above all, the spires of the strange city, set on the top of its mountain, with a deep blue sky for a background, added to the beauty of the scene. It was difficult to imagine that this peaceful country, with its pretty cottages, its innumerable chapels whose bells were then calling its people to worship, and its troops of white-robed men and women answering the summons, was the barbarous Madagascar of twenty years ago.'

CHAPTER II.

ANTANANARIVO, THE CAPITAL.

NOT many years ago comparatively few English people knew anything about Antananarivo. At the outbreak of the late war, writers for the press seemed to think it was on the coast of Madagascar, while others spoke of it as on a river easily accessible from the port of Tamatave. Mistakes such as these are now fast disappearing, and most readers of this book would, if a map of Madagascar were placed before them, look at once in the right direction for the now somewhat familiar name of the capital. To reach it from Tamatave, the chief port on the east coast, a palanquin journey of more than 200 miles through deep forest and over difficult mountain roads must be undertaken. The city is situated in the central plateau, in the highlands of Madagascar, in fact, and is nearly 5000 feet above the level of the sea. It is not exactly in the centre of the island, but is nearer the east than the west coast, though a glance at a good map will reveal the fact that it is to the west of the watershed, the backbone of the central plateau being at a comparatively short distance from the east coast.

The claims of Antananarivo to be the capital of Madagascar are not of very ancient date. For a long

ANTANANARIVO FROM THE NORTH.

time indeed it has been the chief town of Imèrina; but it is not the original capital of even this province. That honour belongs to Ambohimànga, a town picturesquely situated on a well-wooded hill ten or twelve miles north of Antananarivo. In public proclamations the names of Ambohimànga and Antananarivo are often linked together; and it is customary for the sovereign to recognise the claim of the ancient capital by paying it a visit of state once a year, shortly after the new year's festival.

The political influence of Antananarivo is powerfully felt throughout the whole island. In one sense it has a greater relative importance than the capitals of more civilised countries, as it stands almost entirely without rivals. The conditions of society and the present state of civilisation reached by the Malagasy have not led them to congregate in large masses; hence, though village communities abound, there is a singular absence of large towns. Some of the ports, notably Tamatave, are now fast growing in importance, but in the interior of Madagascar there is no other town but that of Fianarantsòa, the capital of the Betsilèo province, that possesses any particular claim to importance, and even this town is very small compared with Antananarivo.

The natives speak with pride of their capital as the very heart of the country. Not only is it the residence of the queen and the centre of the government, but from it go forth the governors who, in the name of the queen, rule the dependent provinces. Constant communication, maintained in the old-world fashion by government couriers, is kept up between the central government and all its dependencies; and a despatch from Antananarivo is a decision from which there is no appeal. Indirectly, too, is the influence—intellectual, moral, and social—of the capital felt even in the remotest districts. The traveller in almost any part of Madagascar will find government officials and traders from Antananarivo or its neighbourhood, and he will soon see what a strong attachment to the native province still exists, and how Antananarivo fashions and customs are followed in these far-off regions.

The name of the capital is derived from two common words—*tanàna*, a town, and *arìvo*, a thousand; and its most probable meaning is, 'The Town of a Thousand.' It might mean 'A Thousand Towns,' but the former meaning is the more likely. The plan of telling off a certain number of settlers to live in some newly-founded town seems to have prevailed widely in Madagascar, and traces of this custom may often be met with. These settlers were called *voànjo* (literally, earth-nuts).

The general appearance of the city as viewed from a distance greatly impresses the traveller. It is built on the ridge and down the sides of a hill nearly two miles in length, and may be seen in some directions from places twenty or thirty miles away. It is, in truth, 'a city set on a hill that cannot be hid.' The crest of the hill is crowned by a group of palaces, and by the house of the Prime Minister, the large glass dome of which glistens in the distance like burnished silver. The sides of the hill are terraced, so that there may be as many as five or six houses one above another; and you may look, not only over a fence into your neighbour's garden, but directly upon the roof of his house on the terrace below you. These terraces are, however, a constant source of trouble and danger. They are built with rough stone, often without much solidity, and, during the heavy rains which fall from November to March, landslips and the falling of retaining walls are of frequent occurrence. After an unusually rainy night, one is sure to hear of some neighbour or friend whose wall has fallen. It will often cost almost as much to build up these retaining walls as to erect the houses for the safety of which they are required. But expense and inconvenience are not the only drawbacks of this system of terracing; serious accidents often occur, and not unfrequently involve loss of life. A little time since a man was buried alive in such a landslip, and no one knew of his death till the body was found by some workmen who were digging away the fallen earth.

The picturesque is not all we should seek in choosing the site of a large city; and though the first sight of Antananarivo, especially to a traveller just getting to the end of a wearisome journey of eight or ten days, and remembering the wretched huts in which he has been compelled to rest on the way, is most welcome, and has often called forth expressions of warm admiration, closer acquaintance with the place somewhat damps the ardour of this admiration, and dispels some of the enchantment lent by distance to the view.

As the weary traveller climbs the steep eastern road, he begins to see that there is a general air of disorder and untidiness about the place. There are indeed roughly-made roads, but they are sadly neglected, and often great chasms eight or ten feet deep are left unfilled for months. Then the houses are perched about in the most irregular fashion. Each house, too, is surrounded by a mud wall; and these walls, though they will stand for years, soon show a tendency to crumble and break down. In addition to this, natives have not our ideas about neatness and the importance of keeping a house in good repair. On all hands may be seen houses either never completed or allowed to fall into a wretched state of dilapidation. Around are many buildings which seem to say of their owners: 'This man began to build, but was not able to finish.' Notwithstanding these drawbacks, however, there are not a few houses that have a comfortable, well-cared-for appearance, and some that look quite gay in the midst of the trees planted around them.

Wonderful changes have taken place in the buildings of the capital within the memory of present residents. An old law formerly prohibited the use of brick or stone within the ancient boundaries of the city. When the queen became a Christian in 1868, this law was abolished, and the consequence is that the city has been almost rebuilt. The Roman Emperor Augustus could boast that he found Rome built of brick, and left it a city of marble. Many of those now living in Antananarivo can say they remember it a town of wood and rushes, and that they have seen it changed into a town of brick and stone, while tiled roofs are gradually taking the place of the old thatched roofs of former times.

This change has had one excellent result : it has lessened the risk of fire. Twenty years ago destructive fires, demolishing in an hour or two twenty, fifty, or even a hundred buildings, were terribly frequent. Now, happily, fires are rare, and when they do occur, the danger of spreading is comparatively small.

Before taking a general survey of the main features of the place, let us cast a glance at the character of the surrounding scenery. To the east the country is extremely broken, only a narrow rice valley dividing the city from the neighbouring hills. These are, except for a few weeks in the depth of the rainy season, bare and brown, and they are deeply scarred by the torrents. Much of the soil is deep red, with masses of granite jutting out in all directions, and in certain conditions of the atmosphere the colouring is very rich ; but, on the whole, the outlook towards the east is not very attractive. On the other sides the country is more open. To the north is the comparatively level and well-populated district of Avàradràno, the ancient capital, Ambohimànga, and the hills near it being among the most noticeable features. To the west and south are very extensive rice plains, looking brown and dreary in the cold season, but during the rains possessing wondrous beauty from the delicate green of the growing rice. Skirting this plain in all directions, or rising like islets from the sea of green, are picturesquely-situated towns and villages in great numbers. Far away to the southwest is the group of the Ankàratra Mountains, rising to the height of nearly nine thousand feet. This is the highest land in Madagascar, and here occasionally the cold is severe enough to produce ice.

But let us take a nearer view of the capital itself. On the whole the impression left on the mind will not be an altogether pleasant one. We must be carried in a simple palanquin, borne by four *màromita*, or bearers, for no vehicle can be obtained. A few horses are used by the richer classes ; but the steep and ill-kept roads, often terribly cut up by the torrents of rain, make riding difficult, and the ordinary mode of locomotion is the palanquin.

As we pass along, we find the roads thronged with dark-skinned foot passengers, most of whom have bare feet and legs, and not a few bare shoulders. Here we may see a party of bearers, sturdy, muscular fellows, laden with hides, which they will carry, slung on bamboos, two hundred miles to Tamatave ; or we may meet others who have just arrived, bearing bales of American calico, or English prints, or tins of paraffin, or loads of flour or sugar, or cases of general merchandise. We shall also be sure to meet women carrying heavy pitchers of water on their heads, or perhaps loads of bricks. In all probability we shall also be shocked by the sight of a gang of men having on their neck and ankles heavy iron rings, connected by long chains. These are the *gàdra-làva*, or convicts, who are chiefly employed in mending roads. By the wayside we shall see here and there roughly-constructed stalls, or *raofia* cloth umbrellas, sitting under which we may observe petty traders offering for sale rice, fruit, meat, eggs of doubtful age, ginger, native sugar, candles, and other small wares. Hanging round these stalls there is sure to be a crowd of half-naked gutter children, and two or three mangy ill-tempered curs, all alike eagerly looking out for any scraps they may be able to pilfer. As we still pursue our journey we may meet a foreigner or two carried in their palanquins, and holding up white umbrellas as a protection against the much-dreaded sunstroke. Or we may hear the thud of many feet, and looking up may see a palanquin coming at full trot, and having a large number of extra bearers and other attendants running at full speed before and after it. In this will be seated some native of rank, probably quite light in colour, and dressed in European costume, the number of his attendants and other followers being a measure of his rank.

As we look around us and examine more minutely the character of this great Hova city, we find how much it lacks that we have been wont to consider essential. We are in a city without streets, at least, in our sense of the term, without shop windows, without railway stations, tram-cars, or cab stands, with no water supply other than that provided by the springs that abound at the base of the hill, and with no sanitary arrangements. The absence of these, however, is less pregnant with evil consequences than it would have been had the town been built on a more level spot. The rainfall is heavy, and during a storm the main roads become watercourses, down which wild torrents rush, carrying with them immense quantities of solid matter. These violent storms are Nature's scavengers, and they help to keep the crowded city in a fairly healthy condition. But typhoid fever exists, and may be expected to increase.

The population of Antananarivo cannot be stated with any accuracy, but the most probable estimate is from eighty to a hundred thousand. A very perceptible increase has taken place within the last twenty years, and the town is still growing. Several districts that were formerly regarded as quite separate are now part of Antananarivo itself.

Among the inhabitants there is always a large floating element, composed of those who come to the capital on government business, or to take part in some law suit. Litigation is very common, and in Antananarivo alone are the higher courts, so that every suit of importance is tried there.

Among the important institutions of Antananarivo we must name the Zomà market, situated at the north-west of the town. As its name Zomà (or Friday) shows, it is properly a weekly market, and though now many traders frequent it daily, only on Friday can the market be seen in all its glory. On Friday mornings country people carrying produce of all descriptions may be seen hurrying from every quarter to Zomà. By ten or eleven o'clock the large open space is crowded, and the people even overflow into the adjoining plain of Anàlakèly, and from the top of Fàravòhitra hill the busy hum of their voices can be plainly heard. Stalls are erected in certain parts of the market, but much of the trade is carried on in the open air. Different trades appropriate different sections of the ground. In one spot we may find timber, and a little above nothing but calicoes and prints. In another part of the market ironwork is offered for sale, and near by is the place where mats of all kinds may be obtained. Yonder is the fruit market, and in another section water-jars and cooking-pots may be bought. One corner of the market has always aroused indignant feelings in the breasts of foreign visitors. It is the slave market. The Government cannot perhaps in the present state of public opinion abolish slavery, although it has done much to mitigate the evils of the system. The public sale of slaves, however, still exists, but we may hope that soon this relic of a non-Christian past will cease to be.

No description of Antananarivo would be complete if it did not contain some account of the way in which Sunday is observed. Here we see an easily appreciated sign of the change the Christian religion is producing among the Malagasy people. Since the beginning of the reign of Rànavàlona II. no markets have been held on this day. A pleasant quiet reigns throughout the town, only broken by the sound of the church-going bell, and by the throngs of well-dressed people going to and from religious services. So fixed is the habit of wearing on Sunday the cleanest and most becoming dress, that Saturday goes by the name of '*lamba*-washing day,' and thus forms an appropriate preparation for Sunday. The dresses of the women are for the most part white or light-coloured, and

D

many of them are handsomely embroidered, and as few of the ladies wear hats or bonnets, their elaborately plaited black hair shows to advantage. Boots and shoes were till recently rarely used, and to a foreigner the sight of bare feet appearing under richly embroidered dresses looked somewhat grotesque.

Antananarivo has recently become so far civilised as to be connected with the port of Tamatave by a telegraph, constructed by a French company. It is now possible for telegrams from London to reach Antananarivo *viâ* Mauritius in two days. An English newspaper (the *Madagascar News*) is published weekly. The editor, Mr. Harvey, though advocating the opening up of the country to commercial enterprise, strongly upholds the cause of national independence. A French paper, called the *Progres de L'Imerina*, advocates what are supposed to be French interests. Two papers in the native language are also published weekly.

To the foreign residents Antananarivo possesses little that can take the place of our public entertainments and amusements. As a newly-arrived French gentleman observed, 'There are no distractions in Antananarivo.' The natives find amusements in such events as the New Year's festival, the annual visit of the queen to Ambohimànga, parade days, great political meetings (or *kabàry*), the setting out of some great man for the coast, or the despatch or arrival of troops. On all such occasions there is an abundant use of gunpowder, and the streets are enlivened by military bands. These attractions draw all classes from their homes, and the roads will be lined for hours with spectators. For the more intellectual, concerts, lectures, and meetings of various descriptions are provided. Then, at certain seasons, school festivals and similar entertainments provide an outlet for the superfluous energy of the younger portion of the population, and by their processions, with the accompaniments of bright dresses, banners, bands of music, import some gaiety into the ordinary dulness of the place.

Perhaps to the list of 'distractions' should be added the weekly opportunity of seeing and being seen, of hearing and imparting news, afforded by the great Zomà market already described; as to the ordinary native, marketing, with all its excitement, its chaffering and its gossip, may safely be numbered among the delights of life.

Antananarivo has been justly deemed by many to be a place of quiet sleepy ways, and when compared with a busy European city this is true enough. But when contrasted with what it used to be, or with any ordinary Malagasy town, it is full of life. There has been a wakening up of new energy, and all around there are visible signs of the changes going on. Religion, education, and commerce have each and all made great strides; and what has already taken place is, we trust, but the promise of greater things to come. From this 'city set on a hill' light is already streaming to all parts of the island.

CHAPTER III.

THE PEOPLE.

THE people of Madagascar, usually spoken of as the Malagasy, are doubtless of mixed origin. That a large African element exists among them cannot be doubted, but speaking generally they are not Africans, but belong to the same family as the Malays and Malayo-Polynesians.

Substantially the same language exists throughout the entire island; and there is not more difference between the dialects than such as exists in our country between the talk of a countryman from Lancashire and another from Somersetshire.

The Rev. L. Dahle, formerly a missionary in the island and now secretary of the Norwegian Missionary Society, thinks that an ancient stratum of African words may be traced that proves an original African settlement in Madagascar, in the same way as the Celtic words in English, even without influencing the grammar, prove that the Celts lived in England before the Anglo-Saxons. But there is now no doubt among those who have studied the question that the Malagasy as spoken to-day is a member of that great group of Oceanic languages that are spoken from Madagascar in the west to Easter Island in the east.

THE PEOPLE.

How the Malayan came to be the predominant language has exercised the thoughts of many. Africa is not more than 300 miles from the west coast of Madagascar, whereas the nearest point of the Malayan peninsula is about 3000 miles away. How came the prevailing element in the population of Madagascar to have been brought from this vast distance? In answering this question we may say, first of all, that there may have been in remote ages land connections which have since disappeared; indeed, many contend that such must have been the case, and that the intervening space was not in those ages, as it now is, a vast expanse of ocean. But even granting the existence of the Indian Ocean in its present form, it may still have been possible for stray canoes to have been carried to Madagascar. The Malays seem to have been a sea-going people, and perhaps some over-venturesome mariners may have set out to the westward, and then have been overtaken by a hurricane and carried by the strong trade wind straight to the east coast of Madagascar. An instructive illustration of the set of wind and current in these parts occurred in the year 1883. Soon after the great volcanic eruption at Krakatoa, on the west coast of Java, in May of that year, vast quantities of pumice were deposited all along the east coast of Madagascar, clearly showing that there is a strong set of wind and current in this direction. So in pre-historic times it is possible that stray canoes may have been carried by the same forces to the same destination.

However the fact is to be accounted for, there

it is—patent to all investigators, and either by force of numbers or by superior intelligence and vigour the Malayan element became the prevailing one so far at least as to cause its language to be used in all parts of the island.

The late Dr. Hildebrant, who after long exploration in Africa went over to Madagascar in 1881, suggested as an explanation of the existence of a stronger African element among the people than is indicated in the language, that probably canoes of warriors from the African coast would often cross to Madagascar, and that these would intermarry with native women and, of course, the children would speak the language of their mothers, and thus the African elements would be largely increased while the language remained substantially unchanged.

Although we are in the habit of speaking of the Malagasy as one people, this seems not to have been a familiar idea to themselves. The free use of the word Malagasy as a generic term for the people is, I think, quite modern; and even yet to some of the natives it is not quite clear what is its exact comprehensiveness. Among themselves the separating tribal names were the common designations in use. Only in recent years has there been anything approaching a unification of the entire island under a central government. The old order, or rather disorder, was that of constant intertribal strife and war, now one tribe and now another proving the stronger.

The chief tribes in the island are the Hova, the Betsilèo, the Bara, the Tankay, the Sihànaka, the Betsimisàraka, the Taimòro, the Taisàka, the Taifàsy, the Tanòsy, the Sakalàva, the Tankàrana. To these might be added many other tribal names of less importance, if we intended to make our list complete.

The Hova are the inhabitants of the central province of Imèrina ; and south of them, still in the central highlands, are the Betsilèo, south and west of whom are the Bara. To the east of Imèrina is the plain of Ankay, already spoken of in Chapter I., and here lives the Tankay tribe. North of these, near Lake Alaotra, are the Sihànaka. Along the eastern coast and for some distance inland dwell the Betsimisàraka. South of these are the Taimòro, the Taifàsy, the Taisàka, the Tanòsy, &c. The great tribe of Sakalàva occupy most of the west coast and part of the north end of the island, in which latter part are also found the Tankàrana.

The Hova are the ruling tribe, and they are essentially a Malayan people with a smaller admixture of foreign blood than any other tribe. They are lighter in colour and quicker in intellect than the other tribes. They have many estimable qualities, and one may form pleasant friendships and enjoy social intercourse with them.

They are keen traders and will go long distances in pursuit of profitable transactions. They have also in some rough fashion managed to make their power as rulers felt throughout nearly the whole of Madagascar. Their rule is oppressive, and they are both hated and feared by the subject races ; but they are a progressive people, ready to assimilate much of our civilisation, and, since their acceptance of Christianity, they have come under influences that are fitting them to take the lead in all that tends to promote the development and well-being of their large island.

The Betsiléo live in the central highlands to the south of the Hova. They are a less advanced people, somewhat timid and easily fleeced and oppressed by their more keen-witted conquerors.

The Bara occupy the land to the south and south-west of the Betsiléo. They are a rough, warlike tribe, very superstitious, and much opposed to all foreign intrusion, whether of the Hova or of Europeans. The Hova power is gradually extending, and mission work is making some slight progress in their country.

The Tankay occupy the long stretch of open country through which the Mangòro flows. They are a quiet pastoral people, and in the dry season many of them earn money as carriers of hides and calico between Ankay and the capital. Mission work has been carried on among them for many years, especially by the Rev. P. G. Peake, of Isoàvina.

To the north of the Ankay plain is the Antsihànaka country. The people of the district are rich in cattle; but they are very degraded and superstitious, and utterly enslaved by their love of the native rum, which they make from sugarcane. Still a very great work, especially in the education of the children, has been carried on here for many years past.

The Taimoro are one of the most remarkable

people in Madagascar. They occupy the coastlands near Mananjara, and are descendants of Arab settlers. They still retain their knowledge of the Arabic letters, and possess sacred books (chiefly containing charms and prayers) in that writing. Many of their religious ideas have been derived from their Arabian ancestors. At present they would not be known from the ordinary Malagasy, and they do not remember the Arabic language. The women among the tribe were always noted for their chastity, and proved the one exception to the prevailing rule. Amongst other tribes a much lower standard exists. The Taisàka, the Taifàsy, and the Tanòsy are also tribes on or near the south-east coast.

The Sakalàva are a wide-spread tribe; and had they been able to combine, they might have held the reins of government in their own hands. Before the time of Radàma I. the Hova paid them tribute. They are a restless and warlike people, and are almost always quarrelling among themselves. They are great slave-dealers, and have supplied the Arab traders with slaves stolen from the interior in exchange for guns and powder. Their gun is their inseparable companion, and it is said that they will not lay it down even to wash their face, but will wash one side of the face first, letting their gun rest meanwhile on the other shoulder. The Sakalàva have been a constant terror to the borderlands of the central plateau, as from among them have come the bands of robbers which have year by year harassed these districts.

The Tankàrana live at the northern end of the

island, in the neighbourhood of the French naval station at Diego Suarez.

It has been estimated that the whole of these tribes do not exceed four millions in number, of which probably about one million may be Hova. There are, however, no accurate data on which to base our calculation.

The dress of the people may next engage our attention. In ancient times this was of the simplest, the men wearing a *saláka*, or loin cloth, and sometimes a sort of shirt called *akànjo;* and the women a *kitàmby*, which was a kind of loose petticoat, and a short close-fitting jacket, also called *akànjo*. Both men and women wear as a loose outer dress the *lamba*.

The *saláka* would usually be of some plain material; but richer men delighted to ornament this portion of their dress with fringes and beads. The *lamba* may be of any plain and cheap material, as hemp cloth, grass cloth, or calico; but for special occasions beautifully woven silk *lamba* of the richest colours are employed. The *lamba* is an article of dress that in the opinion of the ordinary Malagasy is quite indispensable; indeed, to go out of doors without it would be much as if a man went out in his shirt-sleeves, or a woman without her dress.

A change is coming over the people of Antananarivo and its vicinity, and many now use European clothing wholly or in part. Most of the women, however, although adopting a kind of loose dress, and wearing suitable underclothing, and stockings and boots, prefer to retain the *lamba* as their outer garment. As a rule they still go bareheaded, except on long journeys, when they use straw hats as a protection against the sun. Both men and women use umbrellas very freely as sunshades. The love of European clothing is, of course, a stimulus to trade, and many shops have been opened in Antananarivo where the wants of the people can be supplied.

The staple food of the natives is rice, and no meal would be considered satisfactory from which rice was absent. The common saying of the people is: 'There is nothing that will satisfy but rice.' The usual phrase for preparing a meal is 'to cook rice;' and 'to eat rice' means simply to take a meal. The rice is boiled in an earthen pot. English readers must dismiss from their minds all thoughts of milk and eggs, sugar and spice, with which they are accustomed to make their rice palatable. That kind of thing would not suit the Malagasy. What they like is plain well-boiled rice, soft and warm, and they find this like Epps's cocoa, 'grateful and comforting.' It causes a pleasant sensation of fulness and satiety, which they indicate with infinite satisfaction, when they say they are *voky*. To be *voky* (or well satisfied) is to most the acme of delight.

Rice bears a name among the people similar to that we usually give to bread. It is *tohan' ny aina*, the support or staff of life.

But rice, pleasant and satisfying though it be, needs some relish, and the relish, whatever it may be, is called *laoka*. This word originally meant fish; and in some form or other it is found in many of the members of the wide-spread family of the Malayo-Polynesian languages. It has now, however, quite lost this meaning in Central Madagascar, though on the coast fish are called *laokan-drano;* but its survival in this more general sense is interesting, and seems to indicate the fact that the ancestors of the Malagasy came from an island or from the sea-coast.

Laoka may be vegetables or meat, honey, eggs, or milk; stews and curries are also much used, and *ro*, or gravy, is a necessary accompaniment of any well-prepared dish.

The houses of the people differ in different parts of the country. In some parts the bamboo is largely used, in others the *raofia* palm, or the traveller's tree. In Imèrina the red soil of the country well worked into a stiff mud makes durable walls of houses, and till recently was the material most commonly used. The roof may be thatched with leaves or rushes, or dry grass. Rush roofs are the commonest in Imèrina, a rush called *hèrana*, which grows very freely there, forming an excellent and durable thatch.

In recent years a great change has taken place in and around Antananarivo in the style of house building. The use of sun-dried bricks was introduced by the late Mr. J. Cameron, and has been much appreciated by the people. Burnt bricks are also now much used by richer people. Tiles are also rapidly taking the place of thatch, and it seems likely that thatched roofs will soon disappear from the capital.

A modern Antananarivo house is a fairly commodious dwelling. It will have good wooden floors, doors of dark wood, and good glass windows. The walls will be well plastered, and either papered or coloured, often in a pale blue tint, with an ornamental border. Ceilings will be plastered and whitewashed. Furniture of fairly good make is also obtainable.

All native houses till recently were built on one plan. The door was at the south-west corner, and the window at the south-east. The north-east corner was the place of honour, and here stood the wooden bedstead for the heads of the family; this part of the house also bore the name of 'the prayer corner,' as any one offering prayer would turn in this direction. The south-east corner was occupied by the fowls, or by the calf, or the sheep, or the pigs.

Attention to the points of the compass is very marked among the people of Madagascar. They seem never to lose their sense of direction; indeed they may be described with but little exaggeration as 'living compasses.' They apply this sense to the commonest acts of life. You may be asked to pass the book lying to the north of you, or to move your chair a little to the south. A missionary was once told there was a crumb on his northern moustache.

The occupations of the people are becoming more and more differentiated as they advance in civilisation, and we now have smiths, carpenters, goldsmiths, tailors, printers, bookbinders, &c. The separating process is not, however, so fully carried out as among ourselves, as may be illustrated by the fact that I have been accustomed to send to the printing-office when I required the services of a hair-dresser.

The Hova have a great love of trade, and some of them amass what among themselves are regarded as large fortunes, especially those who are able to buy largely of the imported American unbleached calicoes, so much in use among the people throughout the country. They are very keen and hard in driving a bargain. Indeed no one likes to conclude a sale without a large amount of preliminary chaffering called *miády vàrotra* (literally, to fight out a bargain).

A great drawback to the development of commerce is the absence of roads and railways. No wheeled vehicle exists, except a few carts belonging to Frenchmen in or near Tamatave and Mahanòro. A very rough kind of sledge with small wheels is also used in Imèrina for dragging the large slabs of stone used in constructing tombs. With exceptions like these we may say that the Malagasy seem absolutely ignorant of the value of wheels as labour-saving machines. They do not even use horses or mules or oxen to carry goods. Their only beasts of burden are human beings; and men's shoulders have to bear the weight of the thousands of tons of goods that pass between the coast and the interior. Gangs of these porters are met with all along the road, and it is marvellous to see the weights some of them will carry. Men may be seen struggling under loads of cloth, or hides, or salt, weighing 150 or 200 lbs. The carrying of such weights continually often causes unsightly swellings on the shoulders and neck of the porters, which would at once indicate their occupation. The wages for carrying an ordinary load of merchandise between Tamatave and Antananarivo is about twelve or fourteen shillings.

The money used by the Malagasy is the dollar. No other coin is used, except in and near Tamatave, where French money of all kinds circulates freely. Dollars of many kinds are used, and formerly Mexican, Bolivian, Peruvian, and Spanish dollars were readily taken ; but now the dollars of the Latin Union are the only acceptable coins.

For small change these dollars are cut up, and the cut fragments are weighed in small native-made scales. Strange to say, some one must lose fourpence whenever a dollar is cut up. The standard followed in olden times was the Spanish dollar which then weighed more than the French five-franc piece and coins of equal value. The old standard for cut money has remained unchanged, so that while an uncut five-franc piece is worth four shillings, as soon as it passes under the chisel and is cut to fragments its value is only three shillings and eightpence.

CHAPTER IV.

THE GOVERNMENT.

As far back as tradition will carry us there existed in Madagascar a kind of feudalism. Villages were usually built on the hill tops, and each hill top had its own chieftain, and these petty feudal chiefs were constantly waging war with one another. The people living on these feudal estates paid taxes and rendered certain services to their feudal lords. Each chief enjoyed a semi-independence, for no strong overlord existed. Attempts were made from time to time to unite these petty chieftaincies into one kingdom, but no one tribe succeeded in making itself supreme till the days of Radàma I. Andrianampoinimèrina succeeded in bringing the whole of Imèrina under his government; and to his son Radàma he left the task of subduing the rest of the island. By allying himself closely with England Radàma obtained arms and military instructors, and carried war into distant provinces. He ultimately succeeded in conquering many of the tribes, and his reign marks the beginning of a new era in Madagascar. Indeed, only from his days could Madagascar in any sense be regarded as a political unit.

In one direction, however, the result of Radàma's policy must be regarded as retrogressive. Before his reign no chief or king was powerful enough to impose his rule upon the people without their consent, and a large amount of liberty existed. The principal men of each district had to be constantly consulted, and *kabary* (or public assemblies like the Greek *ecclesiæ* or the Swiss communal assemblies) were called for the discussion of all important affairs, and public opinion had a fair opportunity of making itself effective. 'A single tree does not make a forest, but the thoughts of the many constitute a government,' is handed down by tradition as one of the farewell sayings of Andrianampoinimèrina, and is often quoted by the people. This, doubtless, represents the democratic spirit that existed in olden times; but since Radàma I. formed a large army, and a military caste was created, there has always been a strong tendency to repress and minimise the influence of civilians in public affairs, and men holding military rank have wielded the chief authority.

Military rank is strangely reckoned by numbers, the highest officers being called men of sixteen honours; the man of twelve honours would be equal in rank to a field marshal, the man of nine honours to a colonel, and the man of three honours to a sergeant, and so on through the whole series. When any important government business has to be made known, the men from ten honours and upwards are summoned to the palace. Above all these officers stands the prime minister, His Excellency, Rainilaiàrivòny. His father, Rainiharo, gained great power during the long reign of Ranavàlona I., and on his death his two sons, Rainivoninahitriniòny and Rainilaiàrivòny, succeeded him. During the reign of Radàma II. and the early part of that of Rasohèrina, Rainivoninahitriniòny was prime minister and Rainilaiarivòny was commander-in-chief. For some political offence Rainivoninahitriniòny was banished, and for years he was kept in confinement, and for part of the time he wore heavy iron chains. His brother, at the time of his disgrace, united the two offices and titles in his own person, and has been known ever since as prime minister and commander-in-chief. Most Malagasy now try to pronounce these English titles; but when they speak of Rainilaiàrivòny in their own language they are fond of calling him *Ny Mpanàpaka, i.e.* the ruler, or *Ray aman-drenin' ny ambanilànitra, i.e.* father and mother of those under heaven (a common name for the whole people).

The supreme head of the state is the *Mpanjàka*, or sovereign, and every proclamation is issued in her name, and is generally countersigned and confirmed as a genuine royal message by the prime minister. For three reigns, *i.e.*, from the accession of Rasohèrina in 1863, the *Mpanjàka*, has been a woman, and has been the wife of the prime minister. A general impression exists in England that this is an old Malagasy custom; but such is not the case. The arrangement is quite a recent one. The present prime minister (not being of royal blood) is content to be *mpanàpaka*, or ruler; and while all public honour is shown to the queen and her authority is fully acknowledged, those

RAINILAIÀRIVÒNY, PRIME MINISTER OF MADAGASCAR.
(From a Photograph by Captain E. W. Dawson.)

behind the scenes would wish us to believe that the queen is supreme only in name.

As a matter of fact the word of the prime minister, and even his supposed wishes and preferences, are the most potent forces in Madagascar. No one seems able to exercise any independent influence, and time after time men who have shown any special ability or gained popularity have been removed—swept as it were out of the path of the one man who has assumed, and by his ability and astuteness maintained, for thirty years the highest position in the country. Quite recently Ravoninahitriniarivo, formerly one of the ambassadors to this country and to France, died in prison at Ambòsitra, and only in August 1893, Rajoelina, a son of the prime minister, and his son-in-law, Dr. Rajonah, were without any show of public trial sentenced to death on a charge of conspiracy. The death sentence was changed to one of banishment and imprisonment, and these two men, never publicly proved to be guilty, with their wives (one of whom is a daughter of the prime minister) are also in a miserable dungeon near the same town of Ambòsitra. These facts show how absolute is the power of His Excellency the prime minister. Thousands of people sympathised with these condemned men, and still refuse to believe them guilty of the charge laid against them, but no one dared utter a single word of protest. And this is a typical instance of the attitude of the people generally. It is reported that an outspoken young man ventured in some council meeting to make a suggestion which his companions supposed to be distasteful to the prime minister, and at once a cloth was thrown over his head, and those present were ready to hurry him off to prison. There is no doubt a large amount of latent rebellion against this one man government; but those who are most ready to grumble in private will in public be perhaps the most servile of any. In many ways the present prime minister has shown himself an able ruler, and compared with those who went before him he is deserving of great praise. He has made many attempts to prevent the corruption of justice, has strenuously endeavoured to improve the administration, and for many years has managed to hold in check the ambitious projects of French statesmen. He has also many times shown his interest in the cause of education. But he has not done anything to prepare the people for a larger amount of freedom, or to train his subordinates to take their share of responsibility; and one looks around with serious misgiving as to who may be found able to take up the reins of government when he is called to give them up.

Of late years there has been a cabinet composed of eighteen or twenty officers, and the government has been subdivided into eight departments, viz., the army, home affairs, foreign affairs, administration of justice, laws, commerce, finances, and education. At the head of each department is an officer of high rank with several subordinates. The lists of these heads of departments as they are published year by year, might suggest to one not knowing the actual condition of things in Madagascar, an amount of civilisation and of careful attention to the details of government which as a matter of fact do not exist. The heads of departments have very little power, and any one showing a disposition to initiate reforms, or to act with energy in his own department, would soon find himself thwarted and perhaps disgraced. Everything of importance, and indeed many things we should regard as of little importance, are referred to the prime minister. Such over-centralisation is a clog upon the wheels of the political machine, and no business in Madagascar is despatched with promptness. The 'law's delays' have been proverbial all the world over, but in Madagascar they are experienced to a most trying and exasperating degree.

There is little in Madagascar answering to our municipal government. The nearest approach to it is the power exercised at times by the *fokon' olona*, or the people dwelling in any one district. A few years since great energy was shown in this direction, and there seemed a prospect of solid reforms ; but like everything else in Madagascar, the sudden spurt of energy soon subsided into the easy-going *laisser aller* system that seems so congenial to the Eastern mind. Local magistrates known as 'governors' are now placed in most of the provincial towns, and they have power to settle all minor cases, whether criminal or civil.

For the administration of the queen's government among the conquered tribes officers of rank are appointed as *komandy* or governors. The diary of 1894 gives a list of nearly eighty of these governors, who are placed in almost every part of the island. This alone shows how firm a hold the Hova have taken of the country. Would that we could believe the rule of these provincial governors was just and beneficial. No doubt there are good governors, and such could easily be named, but too often the one idea of a man who obtains a provincial governorship is: 'How much can I wring out of my province? I must transmit certain sums to the central government, and I must be sure to send handsome presents to those who are near the throne, or I shall never be safe. All this will require money. Above all, I must not forget to accumulate a fair sum which I may be able to carry to Antananarivo, or my native town in Imèrina.' Thus will the provincial governor reason ; and his actions will correspond with his reasoning. It is notorious that those who are poor when they leave the capital on receiving these appointments frequently return in a few years rich men.

Far from the check of the central government many of these 'little kings' dare to commit acts of tyranny and oppression that would not be possible nearer the capital. I have scarcely ever known a foreigner who had lived long on the coast, or in any of the distant provinces, who did not grow indignant when he began to talk of the doings of the Hova governors he had known. Happy exceptions there undoubtedly are, yet they are but a small percentage of the entire number. This, of course, is not a new thing in the world. The Roman provincial governors, and, indeed, most officials in the good old times, showed the same spirit ; and we must be patient and hopeful, waiting for the better days to dawn for the much oppressed inhabitants of Madagascar.

No account of the government of Madagascar would be complete that did not include some description of the system of '*fanompòana*,' or forced service, which answers very nearly to our old feudal service, and to the system known in Egypt as *corvée*. The tax-gatherer is not the ubiquitous person in Madagascar he is supposed to be among ourselves. There are a few taxes paid by the people, such, for example, as the *isam-pangàdy*, a small tax in kind on the rice crop, and occasionally a small poll-tax; *hàsina*, or money paid to the sovereigns as a token of allegiance, is also paid on many occasions. Taxes of this kind are not burdensome. The one burden that galls and irritates the people is the liability to being called upon at any moment to render unrequited service to the government. Every man has something that may be regarded as his *fanompòana*. The people of one district may be required to make mats for the government; in another district pots may be the article required. From one district certain men are required to bring cray-fish to the capital. Charcoal must be provided by another district, and iron by another, and so on through all the possible series. The jeweller must make such articles as the queen may require; the tailor must ply his needle, and the writer his pen, as the need of the government may be. This system has in it some show of rough-and-ready justice, and is based on the idea that each must contribute to the requirement of the state according to his several ability;

but in its actual working it has a most injurious influence on the well-being of the country. Each man tries to avoid the demands made upon him, and the art of 'how not to do it' is cultivated to a very high degree of perfection.

Sinecures are eagerly sought after, and numbers attach themselves as *dekà* (aides-de-camp) to some great man, so as to avoid the usual claim of feudal service. Many of the head men again make this *fanompòana* system a means of enriching themselves, and require of their subordinates services for themselves as well as for the government.

Many ways present themselves to the fertile brains of these head men. Here is an instance. The *ambonin-jato* (centurion or head man) of a certain district (which for his sake shall be nameless) gives out a notice in the churchyard on Sunday morning, or at the week-day market, that a hundred men will be required next morning to carry charcoal for the government. As a matter of fact he requires only twenty or thirty men; but he knows that many will come to him privately to beg off, and as none will come empty-handed, his profit on the transaction will be considerable.

Another illustration was given me by a British consul. It was customary to send up mails from the coast by government runners; but our English ideas being adverse to demanding unrequited service, the consul had always sent the usual wages to the governor; but this British generosity was quite misplaced in the governor's eyes, and as the consul said: 'He pocketed the dollars and *fanompòaned* the mail.'

A governor in another part of the island some few years ago is said to have made a great haul out of a required levy of soldiers for Solàry, near St. Augustine's Bay. He called the whole body of soldiers under his command (some thousands in all) into the enclosure known as the *rova*. They came little expecting what was in store for them, and were startled to hear the unwelcome news, that they were to be sent to the much-dreaded Solàry. Only a small number were really required; but it is said no one left that enclosure without paying for his personal exemption. A foreign trader present in the town at the time made careful inquiries and calculations, which led him to believe that thousands of dollars had been pocketed by the unscrupulous and money-loving governor.

Illustrations like these might be multiplied a thousandfold, and it is the frequency with which such things occur that makes the well-wishers of Madagascar feel that this unjust system—unjust because of its unequal incidence, and because of the chicanery and oppression it causes—must be swept away before Madagascar can make any true progress. Slavery still exists in Madagascar, and it has its evils, and in some cases these are not light ones; but the total amount of injustice and oppression that springs from the old feudal system is believed to be greater than that arising from slavery. A freeman comparing his lot with that of a slave, will say: 'Are we not all slaves of the sovereign?' And, on the contrary, I have heard slaves refuse to be set free, because they considered themselves better off as they were. A slave only serves his master, and the state can claim nothing from him. He is only a chattel, and his services belong exclusively to his master; but the poor free man is at the mercy of any government official, and never knows what claims will be made upon his service.

Recently a new departure has been made by the government of Madagascar, and the spirit of the people has been chafed by a sudden and unexpected demand for money. The government, owing to the failure of some promised payment by a *concessionaire*, was compelled to raise a large sum of money at very short notice, to meet the claims of the French bank for the half-yearly interest on the loan of 1886. To raise this sum the government ingeniously resorted to the plan of exacting a forced loan or 'benevolence' from all well-to-do people. Sums varying from a few dollars to a thousand dollars were demanded. Receipts were given for these loans; but no interest is to be paid, and nothing was said about repayment. History repeats itself; and an empty treasure chest must be replenished in some fashion. Probably the Malagasy rulers in resorting to this 'benevolence,' were not aware that they were imitating the example of our own Stuart sovereigns and other rulers in bygone times, but were only displaying their own ingenuity. My own impression is that it would not be safe for them to repeat the experiment too often.

CHAPTER V.

THE GROWTH OF THE HOVA POWER, WITH SOME ACCOUNT OF RECENT SOVEREIGNS.

No written history or historical monuments and inscriptions existed among the people of Madagascar when they first became known to Europeans in the sixteenth century, and we are thus entirely dependent on tradition and inference for all our knowledge of their early history. In this chapter I shall give a sketch of one section only of that history, viz. the growth and development of the Hova power.

The Hova believe themselves to have been the conquerors of the Vazimba, whom they represent as having been the original inhabitants of Imèrina; and the ancient graves of the Vazimba were till quite recently regarded as sacred places at which it was common to offer sacrifices. The spirits of the Vazimba were supposed to haunt these places and to have power to inflict bodily ill upon any who offended them.

The names of some of these Vazimba are preserved in old traditional accounts; and after them follow the names of many kings of whom but little is known, until we come to the first sovereign who seems to have any distinct personality, viz. Andrianampoinimèrina, the father of

King Radàma I. He must have begun his reign a little more than a century ago, as he died in 1810, after a reign of twenty or thirty years.

Of all the more important events in the history of Central Madagascar during the past century, *i.e.*, from the reign of Andrianampoinimèrina, we have fairly full and reliable information; and as the unification of Imèrina, and the extension of the Hova dominion into other parts of the island, as well as the closer relations into which the Hova have entered with foreign powers, all fall within this period, we shall confine ourselves to this portion of the history. For fuller details of the traditional history, Ellis's *History of Madagascar* may be consulted.

The following is a list of the *Mpanjàka* or sovereigns of the Hova during the above-named period:—

    1. Andrianampoinimèrina (1785 (?)–1810).
    2. Radàma I. (1810–1828).
    3. Ranavàlona I. (1828–1861).
    4. Radàma II. (1861–1863).
    5. Rasohèrina (1863–1868).
    6. Ranavàlona II. (1868–1883).
    7. Ranavàlona III., whose reign began on July 13, 1883.

Of these seven sovereigns and of the most important events that make their reigns memorable, a short account will here be given.

(1.) **Andrianampoinimèrina.**—Of this remarkable man many stories are told by the natives. His love of justice and his great wisdom are still a theme on which native orators love to dwell, and his example serves them as a goad with which to urge on their audience in right doing. Andrianampoinimèrina seems to have possessed great power of dealing with men; and he succeeded by arms and diplomacy in bringing the whole of Imèrina under his sway. But he accomplished more than this. His soul was stirred by the vision of a united Madagascar; and this ambitious idea, and the urgency with which it was impressed on the mind of the young Radàma, may be regarded as the motive power that set in motion the military undertakings of his descendants. 'The sea is the border of my rice ground,' he was wont to say; and as death began to cast its shadow over him, he solemnly charged his son to carry out the policy indicated by this saying, and to make himself the ruler of a united Madagascar. With succeeding sovereigns this purpose seems to have deepened; and the Hova rule has been gradually extended until now almost the whole of Madagascar is actually ruled in the name of her majesty Queen Ranavàlona III. The ambitious forecast of Andrianampoinimèrina has proved to have been not an idle fancy, but the seed of a policy of extension that has powerfully affected the later history of the island.

Among the fragments of history transmitted by tradition, not one is more valued by the natives than the Farewell Address of this monarch to his young son Radàma, and to his old friends and counsellors to whose care and support he committed him. They often quote it with delight and admiration. It begins with words that indicate a man of a deeply religious mind:—' This is what I say to you all, my relations and friends, for now symptoms of disease have come, for God is taking me away, and that is why I call you together. For now that the command of the Creator has come, and my days are finished, and I am going home to Heaven, behold Ilahidàma, for he is young; and there too are yourselves; for it is only my flesh that will lie buried, but my mind and my spirit will remain with you and with Idàma.

(2.) **Radàma I.**—Radàma I. was son of the preceding. He was not originally intended to be his father's successor; but his elder brother having been detected in a conspiracy against his father's life, Radàma became heir to the throne. Inspired by an ambition that had been kindled and fanned by the dying charge of his father, he set himself to consolidate and extend his power. He has been called 'the enlightened African'; and judging his policy as a whole he may be acknowledged to deserve the name. As a young man he was remarkable among his contemporaries for his temperance and freedom from the common vices; but in later life he exercised little self-restraint, and his end was hastened by his self-indulgences and excesses. Radàma is described as a man of great politeness and winning manners. Captain Le Sage, the first British envoy sent to Antananarivo, was received by him with great courtesy, and was nursed by him during a severe illness with unwearied kindness and care. The one thing that distinguishes Radàma above all his predecessors is that he saw clearly what great advantage he would gain by cultivating friendly relations with the

RADÀMA I.

British government. He was persuaded by the agents of Sir Robert Farquhar, Governor of Mauritius, to sign a treaty abolishing the export of slaves, which up to that time had been carried on vigorously, and was the cause of much misery. As compensation for his losses from the suppression of this profitable traffic he received from the British government an annual grant of money, arms, and military accoutrements, as well as the services of an English sergeant named Brady to drill his soldiers. The name of Brady is still remembered among the people.

The same may be said of the name of Hastie. It was Mr. Hastie who, as agent of Sir Robert Farquhar, successfully negotiated the treaty for the suppression of the slave trade. He continued to reside in Antananarivo, as British agent, till the time of his death in 1826, and was Radàma's trusted friend and adviser. He is still spoken of by the natives as Andrianàsy.

Through the help given him by the British government Radàma succeeded in doing much towards the fulfilment of his father's ambitious projects. He often led his own military expeditions; and he added large tracts of country to his dominions.

(3.) **Ranavàlona I.**—This queen was one of Radàma's wives. She waded to the throne through streams of blood. Like another Athaliah she rose and destroyed all the seed royal. The story of treachery and bloodshed by which her reign was commenced is one of the darkest in the annals of Madagascar.

Ranavàlona was a woman of much sagacity, of great ambition, and of iron will. After a time she reversed Radàma's policy of cultivating friendly relations with the English. She dismissed the British agent, and refused to receive the stipulated subsidy. She did not, however, allow any revival of the exportation of slaves.

The policy of conquest inaugurated by Radàma was carried on with great vigour and with cold-blooded cruelty that has cast a slur upon the history of the Hova power.

Here is one specimen taken from a speech of the Rev. J. J. Freeman in 1837 : 'Ten thousand men not long since were murdered in an afternoon, although they had submitted to the queen, and had taken the oath of allegiance. Their wives and children were dragged into hopeless slavery; but many of them perished on the road, as they were being conducted to the market to be disposed of as cattle. Fifty venerable chieftains, fathers and husbands, were crucified outside one village, and left to perish. Their wives refused to submit to slavery, and were speared on the spot.' *Ex uno disce omnes.* It is well to remember facts like this in estimating the position of the Hova, and their claim to govern the whole of Madagascar. While we freely grant that many benefits have flowed from their rule, we must not forget that they owe their position to conquests such as these ; and they can only vindicate their right to a continuation of their rule by a policy of enlightenment and beneficence.

The reign of the strong-willed queen Ranavàlona

has become famous throughout Christendom on account of her cruel persecution of the Christians; but of this more will be said in Chapter IX.

(4.) **Radàma II.** — Rakòton-d-Radàma (the youth, or young son, of Radàma) was the son of Queen Ranavàlona, born some months after the death of Radàma. The one redeeming feature in the character of queen Ranavàlona I. was the love she showed for her son. Anything Rakòto did was allowable; and strange to tell, he, the beloved son of a cruel and persecuting mother, was often able to shield and deliver the objects of her wrath. At the time of Ranavàlona's illness there existed a rival claimant to the throne in the person of Radàma's cousin, Ramboasalàma. Through the all-powerful aid of the present prime minister and his late brother the succession was secured to Radàma; and a few months later Ramboasalàma died in banishment on his ancestral estate at Ambohimirimo. Whether he was poisoned or starved, or died of chagrin and disappointment, is not known; but from our knowledge of Radàma's character and his horror of bloodshed, we may safely acquit him of all blame in the matter of his cousin's death.

Radàma II. had but a brief reign, and owing to his tragic end he is usually omitted from the list of sovereigns. Those whose all-powerful support made him king became after the lapse of a few months his destroyers.

One of the first acts of this young king on his accession to the throne was to stretch out a hand of friendship to the governments of England and

France, and to proclaim religious freedom throughout his dominions. An embassy, led by Colonel Middleton, was at once despatched from Mauritius to congratulate him on his accession to the throne. A year later special embassies from both the English and French governments were present at his coronation. The enthusiasm that greeted this event seemed to augur well for the brightness and prosperity of his reign; but very soon ominous clouds began to gather, and the reign that had been heralded by such an outburst of gladness ended in a great tragedy. Radàma was strangled at the command of his own officers on May 12, 1863. The causes of his death were his utter misconception of the functions of a ruler, and his want of judgment in putting aside the old and experienced officers who had made him king, and surrounding himself with a band of young counsellors called *Menamàso*. These men shared the fate of their master, and with few exceptions were speared to death.

(5.) **Rasohèrina.**—Radàma II. was at once succeeded by his widow Rabodo, who on becoming queen took the name of Rasohèrina. On accepting the crown she was required by the officers of state to sign a paper containing seven stipulations. These included abstinence from strong drink; the institution of something that seemed much like trial by jury; the abolition of the poison ordeal (*tangèna*); the continuation of religious liberty granted by Radàma, and a solemn declaration that the army, being the 'horn of the kingdom,' should never be broken up.

Rasohèrina never became a Christian, but spite of sundry attempts to reverse the policy of toleration, she firmly maintained it to the end.

During her reign treaties of friendship were successively entered into with England (signed June 27, 1865) and America (signed February 14, 1867). A treaty with France was also under consideration during her reign, but it was not actually signed till some months after the accession of her successor, August 8, 1868. These treaties did much to quiet the country and to allay the constant fears of any breach between the Hova government and any European power. Some time before the French treaty had been signed there had been great tension, and war seemed at one time imminent; but finally the government of Madagascar paid an indemnity of 240,000 dollars for their refusal to confirm the Lambert treaty granted by Radàma.

Just before the death of Rasohèrina Antananarivo was thrown into great confusion by the discovery of a plot to take the reins of government out of the hands of Rainilaiàrivòny, the prime minister, and to place on the throne as successor to Rasohèrina a young prince named Rasàta. The plot failed, and the conspirators were banished. The queen died on Wednesday, April 1, 1868.

(6.) **Ranavàlona II.**—Early on the morning of Thursday, April 2, Ramòma, a first cousin of Rasohèrina, was proclaimed queen under the title of Ranavàlona II.

On her accession it soon became apparent that the attitude of the government towards Christianity was undergoing a change ; and in less than a year (on February 21, 1869) both the queen and the prime minister were publicly baptized. In September of the same year the national idols were burned by the queen's command.

By her character and her actions during the fifteen years of her reign Ranavàlona II. justly deserved the love and esteem in which she was held ; and her death in 1883, just after the outbreak of the war with France, caused such an outburst of genuine sorrow as had never been known in Madagascar before. On the day of her funeral, when after a religious service in the Chapel Royal in Antananarivo, the body was taken to Ambohimànga, the ancient capital, twelve miles away, the road for the whole of that distance was lined with mourners, and funeral dirges were chanted as the *cortège* passed along.

The reign of Ranavàlona II. was marked by events that will always be regarded as great landmarks in the history of Madagascar ; and it is pleasant to think that in her person the name Ranavàlona was redeemed from its evil associations. Ranavàlona II. was as earnest in seeking to advance the kingdom of Christ among her people as Ranavàlona I. had been jealous of the influence of that kingdom, and strenuous in her endeavours to destroy it.

(7.) **Ranavàlona III.**—The present occupant of the throne is the young queen Ranavàlona III., a niece of the last sovereign. She was crowned on Nov. 22, 1883, the twenty-second anniversary of her birthday. Like her two predecessors she is the wife of the prime minister. She came to the throne in troublous times, as the war with France had broken out two months before her accession, on July 13, 1883. She has gained in the esteem of her people and of the foreign residents, as the years have passed, and there is every reason to believe her to be a true Christian, deeply interested in all that tends to elevate her people. Often she has been present at public meetings of special interest, as, for example, the opening of the new hospital at Isoàvinandrìana, and the opening of the new girls' school at Ambòdin' Andohàlo. Her conduct on this occasion was deeply interesting. She had herself been a pupil in the school, when it was carried on in the old building, and she still takes a deep interest in all that affects the prosperity of the school. She had sat patiently through the long opening meeting; and at its close she asked the prime minister to deliver a brief message of congratulation and thanks. When this had been delivered, the meeting was about to be dismissed, when it was observed that her majesty was whispering to the prime minister, and was evidently desirous that something more should be said. Finally she arose, and herself spoke a few kind womanly words of encouragement both to teachers and scholars, and especially urged the latter, above all things, to become true servants of the Lord Jesus Christ.

All classes unite in showing respect to the present queen. She fills her exalted position with becoming dignity. She is credited with being intensely Malagasy in sympathy; and, unless she is much misrepresented, to none of her subjects is the threatened enforcement of a French protectorate more distasteful than to her. What may be her ultimate attitude in regard to this weighty matter remains to be seen.

CHAPTER VI.

THE ANCIENT RELIGION OF THE HOVA.

THE religion of the Hova did not, to a casual observer, present much that seemed likely to predispose them to Christianity. The worship of idols was almost universal. The spirits of ancestors, the sun, moon, and stars, certain sacred mountains and cities, were all appealed to in prayer. Sacrifices of various kinds were offered, sometimes to God, but perhaps oftener to the Vazimba, the spirits of the supposed aborigines, which have already been spoken of.

The fear of witchcraft had immense power, and thousands were destroyed by the *tangèna*, or poison ordeal, by which its presence was believed to be detected.

The *sikìdy*, a kind of divination, and an astrological system called *manàndro*, were largely practised; and a belief in the potency of lucky or unlucky days exercised great influence over the people generally.

Destiny was supposed to be powerful, but certain *fady* (or prohibitions) and sacrifices might, it was believed, turn aside the threatening evil.

Superstition and idolatry prevailed among the people; and yet there was much that helped to gain an entrance for the Christian religion. There was, for instance, no ancient religious literature appealing to the veneration and conservatism of the people. Again, there was nothing exactly answering to the priestly caste that exists in so many lands, and forms a mighty barrier against the entrance of any new religion. Finally, the religion of the Malagasy possessed little cohesion and self-consistency. Apparently derived from various sources and composed of heterogeneous elements, it was never able to present a firm front to the aggressive spirit of Christianity. Hence it had not the power of resistance possessed by many of the more ancient and elaborate religions of the East.

But better than all this, there existed side by side with all the idolatry and superstition, a tradition that a purer religion had once existed, and that the ancient faith of the people had been a simple theism.

The name of God was in constant use. Indeed two names for God were employed by the people —the one *Andriamànitra*—the other *Andriananahàry*. *Andriamànitra* means the Fragrant One, or, in the opinion of some, the Ever Fresh, the Incorruptible. The second name (*Andriananahàry*) means the Creator. The former name (*Andriamànitra*) had been to some extent generalised and degraded, like the Hebrew name *Elohim*, and at times meant little more than mysterious or divine. Parents are called *Andriamànitra*. So too was silk, probably from the use of silk cloths to wrap the dead in. Rice, as 'the staff of life,' also bore the same name. Velvet, strangely enough was called *Zànak' Andriamànitra*, or Son of God. But notwithstanding all this generalising of the meaning of *Andriamànitra*, its prevailing meaning was still the one personal God, and often to prevent misunderstanding, the word was combined with the second name 'the Creator,' so as to show beyond doubt that the Supreme Being was spoken of. In the same way the people often join to the name of God, the strange epithet 'who didst create us with hands and feet'—the hands and feet being taken as specimens of all the physical powers.

This clear recognition of the supreme God, as distinct from, and exalted far above, all idols and spirits, was in itself a great gain, and formed a solid foundation on which to build.

But there was still more; the Malagasy are exceedingly fond of proverbs, and much of the gathered observation and experience of past ages is preserved in these popular sayings. Many of these proverbs are believed by the people to have come down from very ancient times, and are usually spoken of as '*Ohabòlan' ny Ntaolo*,' or Proverbs of the Ancients.

I well remember the delight with which, when I began to collect these old sayings, I found how many of them contained a recognition of God, and some knowledge of His attributes and character; and I think the reader will be pleased to have a few examples and illustrations of this primitive tradition. The dwelling-place of God was believed to be in heaven, hence a strangely worded proverb says: 'Like a little chicken drinking water; it looks up to God.' God was confessed to be greater than the imagination of man can conceive; thus another proverb says: 'Do not say God is fully comprehended by me.' God's omniscience was recognised in the words, 'God looks from on high and sees what is hidden;' and again in the following: 'There is nothing unknown to God, but He intentionally bows down His head (that is, so as not to see);' a very remarkable parallel to St. Paul's words: 'that the times of ignorance, therefore, God overlooked.' Again, God's omnipresence was implied in an extremely common saying: 'Think not of the silent valley' (that is, as affording an opportunity for committing a crime); 'for God is over our head.' God was also acknowledged as the author of life, as the ordinary phrase used in saluting the parents of a newly-born child, was: 'Salutation! God has given you an heir.' Another proverb speaks thus of God's power to control the restless will of man: 'The waywardness of man is controlled by God; for it is He who alone commands.' God was the rewarder both of good and evil; and so they have the saying: 'God, for whom the hasty wait not, shall be waited for by me.' 'Let not the simple one be defrauded; God is to be feared;' 'God loves not evil;' 'It is better to be held guilty by man than to be condemned by God.' These are simply examples, and their number might be easily augmented, but they are enough to show that God did not leave Himself without witness.

Having such ideas as to the Divine Being, what could the people be said to know as to their own moral and spiritual nature?

Though their ideas of the spirit are vague, there is a clear recognition of it as distinct from the body. The spirit is called *fanàhy*, a noun derived from a root *ahy*, which means care, or solicitude; or more probably from *naly*, which signifies will or intention. That the spirit survived the body is clearly implied in all the beliefs of the people concerning ghosts, and in their prayers to their ancestors. The speech of Andrianampoinimèrina, from which I have quoted, contains the following words: 'It is my body that will lie buried; but my spirit will be with you to whisper to you words of counsel.'

As to the conscience, I am sorry I cannot say much. The ideas of right and wrong are usually expressed by *mety* and *tsy mety*, which do not mean much more than proper and improper. For the conscience no name exists; the nearest approach being *fieritrerètana*, which means meditation, or the faculty of meditating. The hope is that this word, like so many others, having received a Christian baptism, will now gradually gain a deeper meaning. But the fact remains that no distinct name for conscience was ever needed in pre-Christian times; and this is, I fear, a sign of an undoubted lack in the nature of the people. I do not, however, wish to imply that they are altogether without a sense of right and wrong; but merely that their ideas are vague and shadowy. This is, perhaps, the very thing that we should look for in such a people. It has been the special fruit of Christian teaching that it has awakened the conscience.

Enough has been said to show that a missionary

to Madagascar can use as the groundwork of his teaching much that already existed in the old religious beliefs of the people. He can, and does constantly claim to be, not 'a setter forth of strange gods,' but a herald of that one God, who made us all, and to whom the ancestors of the people had been accustomed to pray from time immemorial.

In another chapter we shall show how this knowledge of God, so marvellously kept alive through all the ages of idolatry and superstition, has now been lit up with new meaning, and has begun to exercise a more potent influence than it ever did in the past.

CHAPTER VII.

THE INTRODUCTION OF CHRISTIANITY.

WITHIN a short time of the discovery of Madagascar in 1506 the Portuguese made an attempt to convert the natives to the Roman Catholic faith. Their endeavours, however, were but of brief duration, and produced no permanent result.

In the following century French Roman Catholic missionaries laboured for nearly twenty years in and near Fort Dauphine. The names of the first two missionaries were Nacquart and Gondrée, and they reached Fort Dauphine in 1648, during the governorship of Flacourt. A catechism prepared by these early French missionaries was published by Flacourt in 1657. The fruits of this French mission were but small, and owing to the arrogance and violence of the over-zealous missionary, Father Stephen, he was massacred by the natives, and the work of evangelising the people was abandoned.

Protestant missions in Madagascar date from 1818. For some years before this, however, Madagascar had been engaging the thoughts of the directors of the London Missionary Society. One of its first missionaries to South Africa, the celebrated Dr. Vanderkemp, took the deepest interest in the island. Immediately after his arrival he began to collect information, and to urge the sending out of missionaries. In 1808 he writes about 'the long-neglected island of Madagascar'; two years later he again urges the sending of missionaries to 'our newly-acquired conquest,' all

DAVID JONES.

the French establishments on the coast of Madagascar having fallen to us in 1810 upon our taking the island of Mauritius, of which they were considered dependencies.

Dr. Vanderkemp had himself planned to lead the new mission, and preparations were far advanced, when his death in 1811 caused a temporary abandonment of the idea.

The men to whom the honour of being the pioneers of Protestant missions in Madagascar belongs were two Welshmen, named David Jones and Thomas Bevan. They were fellow-students in

DAVID GRIFFITHS.

a theological school or seminary in Cardiganshire. This was the 'Ysgol Neuaddlwyd,' or school of Neuaddlwyd, not far from the town of Aberayron, founded by the Independent ministers of Cardiganshire in 1810.

The principal of this 'school' was Dr. Phillips,

a preacher of great power, an earnest Christian worker, and a man deeply interested in missions. Strange to say, the first volunteers for mission work in Madagascar were led to offer themselves to the Society through a dream of their tutor. Dr. Phillips had been reading much about Madagascar, and his mind was so deeply stirred, as he thought of the wretchedness of the people and their need of the Gospel, that he could not rest. The next morning he related his dream to the assembled students, and asked: 'Now, who will go as a missionary to Madagascar?' From the far end of the school, without any hesitation, came from the lips of David Jones the reply: 'I will go'; and immediately this was followed by a similar offer from his fellow-student Thomas Bevan. Thus these two Welsh students became the first Protestant missionaries to the Great African Island. Wales may well praise God for the links that bind her to the cause of Jesus Christ in Madagascar, since she had much to do with the laying of the foundation of the great work that has been carried on there. David Jones and Thomas Bevan were not her only contribution; but later on David Griffiths (1821) and David Johns (1826), both, like the pioneer missionaries, students of Dr. Phillips at Neuaddlwyd, were earnest and successful missionaries in the same land.

The first mission party was overtaken by a terrible disaster. After a preliminary visit by the missionaries alone, during which they had become fully convinced of the capacity of the people to receive education, they resolved to settle in Madagascar at once with their wives and their two young children.

Mr. and Mrs. Jones and their child arrived in Tamatave on October 13. When Mr. and Mrs. Bevan and their child reached the harbour early in January the sad news met them that Mrs. Jones and her infant were both dead, and that Mr. Jones himself was believed to be dying. This news had such a depressing effect on Mr. Bevan that he expressed his firm conviction that he too would certainly die, a prophecy too soon to be fulfilled. Within a few days his child sickened and died; then he himself was taken ill, and died on January 31, and three days later Mrs. Bevan also died. Mr. Jones was thus the only survivor out of that party of six. They had not sufficiently thought of the danger of taking up their residence at the beginning of the rainy season, and were, no doubt, poorly housed, and thus they fell easy victims to the deadly climate of the coast.

Mr. Jones, though greatly weakened by fever, refused to abandon the hope of evangelising Madagascar. He returned for a time to Mauritius to recruit his strength; and in 1820 he once more started for Madagascar—this time in company with Mr. Hastie, the British Resident, and not to settle on the coast, but in the capital of King Radàma. In this purpose he was encouraged by Sir Robert Farquhar, the governor of Mauritius, and one of the best friends Madagascar ever had.

Radàma received Mr. Jones kindly, and gave him permission to settle in Antananarivo; and a firm friendship sprang up between him and the king, which lasted till the death of the latter eight years afterwards.

It is characteristic of the shrewdness of King Radàma, that in giving permission for missionaries to reside in his country he expressly stipulated that some of them should be skilled artisans, so that his people might be instructed in weaving, smith's work, carpentering, &c. To this request the Society wisely acceded, and a number of Christian artisans were sent out.

The names of some of these are still remembered in Madagascar—*e.g.*, Mr. Canham, the tanner, Mr. Chick, the smith, Mr. Rowlands, the weaver, and, above all, Mr. Cameron, whose mechanical skill and great practical ability won for him the regard and confidence of the people, and whose love for the Malagasy led him to return to the country after the persecution, and to remain there till his death in 1875.

The influence of these artisans was of immense value; and to their teaching is to be attributed much of the skill of the Malagasy workmen of to-day. There is no doubt that the manifest utility of their work did much to win for the mission a measure of tolerance from the still heathen rulers of the country.

One instance of this is given by Mr. Cameron in his *Recollections*. Soon after the dismissal of Mr. Lyall, the British agent, Queen Ranavàlona was beginning to feel uneasy about the growing influence of foreign ideas, and wished to get rid of the missionaries. She sent some officers to carry her message, and the missionaries were gathered together to meet the queen's messengers, and were told that they had been a long time in the country and had taught much, and that it was now time for them to think of returning to their own land. The missionaries, alarmed at this message, answered that they had only begun to teach some of the elements of knowledge, and that very much remained to be imparted. They mentioned sundry branches of education, among which were the Greek and Hebrew languages, which had already been partially taught to some. The messengers returned to the queen, and soon came back with this answer: 'The queen does not care much for Greek and Hebrew. Can you teach something more useful? Can you, for instance, teach how to make soap?"

This was an awkward question to address to theologians; but after a moment's pause Mr. Griffiths turned to Mr. Cameron and asked him whether he could answer it. 'Give me a week,' said Mr. Cameron, and the week was given. At its close the queen's messengers again met the missionaries, and Mr. Cameron was able to present to them 'a bar of tolerably good and white soap, made entirely from materials found in the country.' This was an eminently satisfactory answer, and the manufacture of soap was forthwith introduced and is still continued to the present day, though no one would now venture to call the soap 'white.'

As a result of the making of this bar of soap the mission gained a respite of about five years, during which the queen still tolerated the presence and teaching of the missionaries for the sake of the material advantages derived from the work of the artisans; and it was during these years that the first churches were formed, and the

Christian religion began to take deep root among the people.

The education of the young naturally formed an important element in the work of the mission from its commencement, and under the patronage of King Radàma I. the work flourished greatly. Radàma never became a Christian. 'My Bible,' he would say, 'is within my own bosom.' But he was a shrewd and clever man, and his ideas had been much broadened through intercourse with foreigners, and especially through his constant intercourse with Mr. Hastie, the British agent, and he clearly saw that the education of the children would be an immense gain to his country. Thus he did all in his power to further this branch of missionary work, and both he and Mr. Hastie showed great interest in the prosperity of the schools.

In the year 1826 about thirty schools had been founded, and there were nearly 2,000 scholars; in 1828 the schools were forty-seven, but the number of scholars had fallen to 1,400. At one time the missionaries reported 4,000 as the number of scholars enrolled, though there were never so many as this actually learning. During the fifteen years the mission was allowed to exist (1820–1835) it was estimated that from 10,000 to 15,000 children passed through the schools, so that when the missionaries were compelled to leave the island, there were thousands who had learned to read, and who had by the education they had received been raised far above the mass of their heathen fellow countrymen.

The direct spiritual results of the missionaries' work were of slow growth, and it was not till eleven years after Mr. Jones' arrival in the capital that the first baptisms took place. This was on Sunday, May 29, 1831, in Mr. Griffiths' chapel at Ambodin' Andohàlo, when twenty of the first converts were baptized in the presence of a large congregation. On the next Sunday, June 5, eight more were baptized by Mr. David Johns in the newly-erected chapel at Ambàtonakànga.

From this time the growth was comparatively rapid and encouraging, and by the time of the outbreak of persecution two hundred had been received into the membership of the two churches that were formed.

Summing up the results of the fifteen years' work, Messrs. Freeman and Johns say :—

'During the fifteen years already mentioned the whole of the Scriptures of the Old and New Testaments were translated, corrected, and printed in the native language at the capital, aided by very liberal grants from the British and Foreign Bible Society. Not fewer than 25,000 tracts, aided by the prompt and generous encouragement afforded by the Religious Tract Society, were printed ; Russel's Catechism was translated, and an edition of 1,000 copies generously given by Mr. Cameron, a member of the mission. Nearly all these publications were put into circulation. The number of schools increased till they amounted to nearly 100, containing nominally about 4,000 scholars, to whom were imparted the elements of instruction and of religious truth. Probably 10,000 or 15,000 altogether passed through the mission schools during the period under review. Elementary books were provided for the use of these, and probably as many more were distributed among those who voluntarily acquired the art of reading without attendance on the mission schools.

'Two printing-presses were established at the capital by the London Missionary Society. A dictionary of the language was prepared and printed in two volumes, the first embracing the English and Malagasy, and the other the Malagasy and English. Two large congregations were formed at the capital. Nearly 200 persons, on a profession of their faith, applied for admission to church fellowship, and numerous week-day evening services were established at the dwelling-houses of the natives. Adult Bible classes were started for the perusal and examination of portions of the sacred Scriptures. Various preaching stations were visited every Sabbath in several towns and villages, at which schools existed, more or less distant from the capital. Many of the principal scholars had their attention for a long time directed to the English language and became familiar with the English Scriptures. Innumerable opportunities were embraced of conversing with the natives. With many of them habits of intimacy and friendship were formed, and as the result of these and many other subsidiary means, the minds of multitudes, it may be affirmed, became in *some* degree enlightened in the truths of Christianity, and so far affected by what they knew as to renounce many of the superstitious customs of the country.'

CHAPTER VIII.

THE QUARTER OF A CENTURY WHEN 'THE LAND WAS DARK.'

THE story of the persecution and sufferings of the Malagasy Christians has often been told, notably in the *Narrative* of Freeman and Johns, and later by the Rev. W. Ellis in his *Martyr Church*. An excellent epitome may be found in the recently published *Story of the L. M. S.*, by the Rev. C. Silvester Horne, M.A. In this chapter the briefest sketch possible must suffice.

I have taken as a chapter heading the translation of a phrase commonly used by the Malagasy Christians when they speak of the persecution. It was *ny tàny maizina*, the time when the land was dark. The phrase is often on their lips, and the story of the sufferings and fidelity of the martyrs is one they will never allow to be forgotten.

For us too the story has an undying interest, and as one of the most thrilling episodes in the history of the London Missionary Society the main facts should be kept well to the front for the instruction and encouragement of the present generation.

The causes that led to the persecution are not far to seek. They were, on the one hand, an intensely conservative clinging to ancestral customs and to the idols in which their fathers trusted, and on the other hand a suspicious and jealous fear of foreign influence. The zealous work of the missionaries was believed by many of the queen's advisers to be only a cloak to conceal political designs. A new power had arisen in the land. The teaching of the foreigners was proving so attractive that their chapels were crowded, and the influence of the new religion was making itself felt in many families. Whither would all this lead ? Was it not possible that these foreigners were simply seeking to gain the affections of the people that they might pave the way for the ultimate annexation of the island by the English government ? There was nothing unreasonable in such suspicions. Our ships were often seen in the ports of Madagascar, and at one time we had some claim to districts on the coast. We were known to be a people prone to extend our power into foreign lands ; and why should we be credited with pure philanthropy in these efforts to win the goodwill of the Malagasy ? An amusing story is told in illustration of this suspicion and jealousy. The word 'society' had been introduced by the missionaries as the name of some combination for mutual help in times of sickness and trouble. Now 'society' to a native ignorant of English would suggest a phrase of their own which sounds very much like it, viz., *sosay atj*, ' push (the canoe) over this way.' This to the ingenious and suspicious mind of the hearers suggested the idea of pushing over the government of Madagascar to those across the ocean, who were supposed to be greedily seeking to seize it. All this sounds absurd, but nothing seems too ridiculous to obtain credence among an excited and suspicious people.

The outbreak of violent opposition to missionary teaching and influence was delayed for several years, because the queen and her ministers valued so highly the work of the missionary artisans. The missionaries knew they could not depend upon any long continuance of the freedom they had hitherto enjoyed. But before the actual outbreak of persecution they were greatly cheered by signs of a deep spiritual work. A spirit of prayer began to manifest itself, and week evening meetings conducted by the natives themselves were held in private houses. A letter reporting these encouraging signs was written in November 1834; but before the few remaining weeks of the year had passed away, the storm burst. The first sign of a change was a proclamation forbidding any person to learn to read and write except in the schools established by government. Much uneasiness was felt by the missionaries, and many things seemed to show that active opposition would not be long delayed.

Towards the close of January 1835 one of the queen's officers presented a formal complaint against the Christians, comprising the following six points:—

(1.) They despise the idols of the land.

(2.) They are always praying; they hold meetings in their own houses for prayer, without authority from the queen; and even before and after meals they pray.

(3.) They will not swear by the opposite sex (according to the usual custom of the country), but, if required to swear, merely affirm that what they say is true.

(4.) Their women are chaste, and therefore different customs from those established in the country are introduced.

(5.) They are all of one mind respecting their religion.

(6.) They observe the Sabbath as a sacred day.

Happy the people against whom no worse charge could be laid!

Soon after this the queen, on passing a native chapel during service time and hearing the singing, was heard to say: 'They will not stop till some of them lose their heads.'

Excitement increased, and opposition to the new teaching grew bolder. One chief of rank is reported to have sought an audience with the queen and to have spoken to her thus: 'I am come to ask your majesty for a spear, a bright, sharp spear—grant my request.' He would rather kill himself, he said, than live on to see the idols of his fathers dishonoured.

On Thursday, February 26, 1835, a formal letter was sent to the missionaries telling them that they could no longer be allowed to instruct the natives in the Christian religion. At four o'clock that afternoon the usual public service was held in the chapel at Ambàtonakànga, and one of the natives was requested to deliver an address. The chapel was quite full, and the address was excellent, founded on the very appropriate text, 'Save, Lord, we perish.' It was the last public address ever delivered there.

Three days later, viz. on Sunday, March 1st, the edict publicly prohibiting the Christian religion was delivered in the presence of thousands of the people who had been summoned to hear it. The place of meeting was the plain of Imahamàsina, the Champs de Mars of Antananarivo, an open space lying to the west of the long hill on which the city is built, and large enough to contain one or two hundred thousand people. In the middle of the plain crops up a large mass of granite rock, on which only royal personages are allowed to stand. Hence, probably, the name Imahamàsina, which means 'having power to make sacred.' Here, from time to time, large public assemblies have been held, but never one of higher significance or of more far-reaching issues than that of Sunday, March 1st, 1835.

Of this great *kabàry* notices had been sent far and wide. All possible measures had been taken to inspire the people with awe, and to make them feel that a proclamation of unusual importance was about to be published. The subjects of Ranavàlona had often been awe-stricken by the cruelty and determination of their sovereign. We have seen the kind of measures by which her throne was obtained. But now she seemed anxious to make her people feel that her anger was burning with an unwonted fury. Hence the steps taken to secure the attendance of all classes of the community, not even invalids being excused.

'Morning had scarcely dawned,' we are told,

'when the report of the cannon, intended to strike awe and terror into the hearts of the people, ushered in the day on which the will and the power of the sovereign of Madagascar to punish the defenceless followers of Christ was to be declared. Fifteen thousand troops were drawn up, part of them on the plain of Imahamàsina, and the rest in two lines, a mile in length, along the road leading to the place. The booming of artillery, from the high ground overlooking the plain, and the reports of the musketry of the troops, which was continued during the preparatory arrangement for the *kabàry*, produced among the assembled multitudes the most intense and anxious feelings.

'At length the chief judge, attended by his companions in office, advanced and delivered the message of the sovereign, which was enforced by Rainiharo, the chief officer of the government. After expressing the queen's confidence in the idols, and her determination to treat as criminals all who refused to do them homage, the message proceeded: "As to baptism, societies, places of worship, and the observance of the Sabbath, how many rulers are there in the land? Is it not I alone that rule? These things are not to be done. They are unlawful in my country," says Queen Ranavàlona, "for they are not the customs of our ancestors."'

As a result of this *kabàry* four hundred officers were reduced in rank, and fines were paid for two thousand others, and thus was ushered in a persecution that lasted a quarter of a century.

The missionaries were compelled to leave the

island. But they had done a work the results of which were not to be destroyed even by Queen Ranavàlona. They had imparted much general knowledge, and had trained up many skilled workmen, they had taught some 10,000 or 15,000 children in their schools, and it was estimated that altogether 30,000 people had learned to read; they had reduced the language of the Hova to a written form; they had translated the Bible, and prepared elementary school books; they had gathered in the first fruits of their labours, and had been able to found several small Christian churches. The work had just begun to give them abundant reason for hopefulness, when all their bright anticipations were clouded over, and the continuance of their work was made impossible. The last party of missionaries, consisting of the Rev. D. Johns and Mr. Edward Baker, sorrowfully bade farewell to Antananarivo in July, 1836.

And now, to use again the familiar native phrase, the 'land was dark' for twenty-five years, and the Christians were called to suffer the severest persecution. Queen Ranavàlona (the Queen Mary of Madagascar), with all the force of her strong will set herself to destroy the new religion. 'It was cloth,' she said, 'of a pattern she did not like, and she was determined none of her people should use it.' The victims of her fury form a 'noble army of martyrs' of whom Madagascar is justly proud.

The proto-martyr of the island was Rasalàma, a young woman, who was put to death at Ambòhipòtsy on August 14, 1837. She quietly knelt down to commend her soul to God, and while she was still praying her life was taken by the spear of the executioner.

The measures taken to destroy Christianity were not at all times equally severe. The years that stand out with special prominence in the annals of the persecution are 1835–37, 1840, 1849, and 1857.

Of what took place in 1840 we have recently had, in a letter written at the time by the Rev. D. Griffiths, who was then residing in Antananarivo, and published in *News from Afar* (Feb. 1895), a graphic story told by an eye-witness. The nine condemned Christians were taken past Mr. Griffiths' house. 'Ramanisa,' he says, 'looked at me and smiled; others also looked at me and "their faces shone like those of angels," in the posture of prayer and wrestling with God. They were too weak to walk, having been without rice or water for a long time.

'The people on the wall and in the yard before our house were cleared off by the swords and spears of those conducting them to execution, that we might have a clear, full, and last sight of them. They were presented opposite the balcony on the road and at the entrance of the yard for about ten minutes, carried on poles by the executioners, with merely a hand-breadth of *jabo* cloth to cover them. They were then led away to execution . . . .

'The cannon fired to announce their death was shattered to pieces and the gunner's clothes burnt, which was considered fearfully ominous, many whispering, "*Thus will the kingdom of Ranaválo-manjàka be shattered to pieces.*"'

In 1849 what may be called the great persecution

took place. Not less than 1900 persons suffered punishment of various kinds—fines, imprisonments, chains, or forced labour in the quarries. Of this number eighteen suffered death—four of noble birth by being burnt at Fàravòhitra, and fourteen by being thrown over the great precipice of Ampamarinana (*lit.* the place of hurling).

It is not easy to estimate exactly the number of those who suffered the punishment of death in these successive outbursts of persecution. The most probable estimate is that the victims were between sixty and eighty. But these formed only a small portion of the total number of sufferers. Probably hundreds of others died from the burden of their heavy iron chains, or from fevers, or severe forced labour, or from privations endured during the time they were compelled to hide in caves or in the depths of the forest.

Notwithstanding the severity of the persecution, however, much quiet Christian work was carried on in the lulls between the storms. Meetings were held in secret, sometimes far away in the forest, sometimes on hill-tops, sometimes in lone country houses, sometimes in caves, or even in unfinished tombs. Thus was the story of the Covenanters repeated and the impossibility of destroying Christian faith by persecution again shown. Through the long years of persecution the Christians were constantly receiving accessions to their ranks, and the more they were persecuted, 'the more they multiplied and grew.'

CHAPTER IX.

THE RENEWAL OF MISSIONARY WORK.

THE dreary years of waiting and of hope deferred at length came to an end. Queen Ranavàlona had a long reign of thirty-three years, but in 1861 it became evident to all that she would not reign much longer. From native accounts we learn the details of her last days. 'The aged queen had for some time been suffering in health. Diviners had been urgently consulted, and charms and potent herbs had been employed, but with no avail, and late in the summer of 1861 it became generally known that the fatal moment could not long be delayed.' Mysterious fires were said to be seen on the tops of the mountains surrounding the capital, and a sound like music was heard rising from Isòtry to Andohàlo. The queen eagerly questioned those around her as to the meaning of these portents. One replied: 'It is not the fire of men, but the fire of God.' Others more boldly spoke of these signs as foreshadowing death. But while the dying queen was anxiously praying to the idol in whom she put her trust, there were those who whispered to the prince that the fire was 'the sign of Jubilee to bring together the dispersed and to redeem the lost.' And so the event proved. The aged queen passed away during the night of Friday, August 15, and early on the morning of August 16 the news spread rapidly through the capital, and her son was proclaimed as Radàma II. One of the first acts of the new sovereign was to proclaim religious liberty. The chains were struck off from the persecuted Christians, and the banished were recalled. Many came back who had long been in banishment or in hiding, and their return seemed to friends, who had supposed them long dead, like a veritable resurrection. The joy of the Christians was intense. The long season of repression had at last come to an end, and now it was no longer a crime to meet for Christian worship or to possess Christian books. On that first Friday evening some of the older Christians met in a house at Anàlakèly and spent the night in prayer and praise and in reading through the whole of Jeremiah, a book which seems to have possessed special attractions for the persecuted church. Sunday services were begun in eleven private houses; but soon these small congregations were consolidated, and three large congregations formed at Ambàtonakànga, Ampàribè, and Anàlakèly.

Radàma II. eagerly welcomed intercourse with foreigners, and gave the Christians permission to write at once urging that missionaries should be sent out. He himself also wrote to the London Missionary Society making the same request. The Rev. John Lebrun, son of the venerable missionary who was at that time still living in Mauritius, paid a short visit to the capital to encourage the Christians and to assure them that they would speedily receive the much desired help. Mr. Ellis left England on Nov. 20, and remaining in Mauritius during the rainy season, arrived at Antananarivo in June, 1862. The directors with great promptness arranged to send out a band of missionaries in the spring. These were duly appointed, and on April 15 they sailed from London in the *Marshal Pelissier*, a vessel belonging to a line of merchant ships known from the colour of their paint as the 'pea-soupers.' The party consisted of the Rev. Robert Toy and Mrs. Toy, the Revs. John Duffus and William E. Cousins, Dr. Andrew Davidson and Mrs. Davidson, Mr. John Parrett (missionary printer) and Mr. Charles H. Stagg (school-master). The vessel also carried 10,600 copies of the New Testament and portions of the Old Testament, the generous grant of the Bible Society; 3000 reams of printing paper, the gift of the Religious Tract Society, 20,600 volumes of tracts and Christian books (such as *Come to Jesus*, *The Anxious Inquirer*, *The Pilgrim's Progress*, lesson books, arithmetics, &c.), a store of medicines and of school materials, and a small printing-press. These missionaries arrived in Tamatave on August 9, and reached Antananarivo in two parties on August 28 and September 2, about twenty weeks after sailing from London.

We (for I find it more convenient to use the first person), received a most hearty and loving welcome from the native Christians. On the first Sunday after our arrival (September 7), it was thought well to celebrate the renewal of missionary work by holding a united Communion Service. This was held at Ampàribè. The church members from the three congregations nearly filled the rough unsightly building, which then stood where the present school-house has since been built. The building was composed chiefly of a roughly made rush roof resting upon the mud walls surrounding the plot of ground on which the original place of meeting (Rainikoto's house) stood. But notwithstanding the meanness and unsightliness of the building, and the strangeness, and even grotesqueness, as it might appear to some, of the dress and general appearance of many of those gathered together there, to those of us who had travelled so many hundred miles over sea and land in the hope that we might help forward God's work in the island, the service was one of profound interest, and awoke in our hearts fresh thankfulness and hope. Had the same people attempted to meet for worship a little more than twelve months earlier, many would have lost their lives; now in open daylight they were assembled in this happy service, none daring to make them afraid. There were present between 700 or 800 communicants. When the first mission was broken up in 1835, the number of communicants was estimated at about 200. For twenty-five years had Queen Ranavàlona been persecuting the Christians; many had died as witnesses for Christ, and many more had suffered in other ways for His sake; but now, a year after the queen's death, there were nearly four times as many professed followers of Christ in the capital alone as there had been in all the churches when the first missionaries were compelled to leave the island.

The probable number of Christians in Madagascar on our arrival in 1862 was between 5000 and 7000 ; and there were, in addition to the three city congregations, about twenty or twenty-five small gatherings in different towns and villages around.

The eagerness of the people to learn at this time was intense, and we were beset from morning to night by crowds of visitors. We had tried hard to learn Malagasy on board ship, but found the guidance of Griffiths' Grammar somewhat the reverse of helpful ; but from the day of our landing in Tamatave we spent our time in almost uninterrupted intercourse with the natives. In this way we speedily enriched our vocabulary, and with the help of some of our friends who could speak English (notably the present Governor of Tamatave, Rainandriamampàndry, and his brother, Rabeàrana), we soon began to see light where all had been darkness. With the characteristic eagerness and rashness of young men we wished at once to make use of what we had acquired, and after a few weeks we began to deliver short addresses. My own first attempt was made at Anàlakèly on October 5, 1862, the fifth Sunday after my arrival in Antananarivo. The eagerness of the people to attend religious services in those early days was wonderful. It seemed as if they could not spend too many hours in the house of God. After so many years of persecution, during which all meetings had to be held with the greatest secrecy, the enjoyment of sitting in broad daylight, listening to God's Word, joining in prayer, and, above all, singing their hymns without the dread of some

RAINANDRIAMAMPANDRY, GOVERNOR OF TAMATAVE.

enemy overhearing and denouncing them, seemed to afford the most intense delight. Often they would be at church by six or seven o'clock and would remain till eleven, and then, after about two hours, would return and stay till sunset. I have heard as many as five or six distinct addresses given during one morning service.

Schools were in those days non-existent, with the exception of what was called the King's School in the stone palace at Ambòhipòtsy, where a few lads belonging to the upper classes received some slight teaching. Books, of course, were very scarce. Happy was he who possessed a few leaves of a Testament, or part of a Psalter, or a Hymn Book or Catechism, soiled and ragged though it might be. Very few complete Bibles remained, not more than a dozen or so; and these, thumb-worn and patched as they were, were regarded as priceless treasures.

Great disappointment was expressed on our arrival that the expected Scriptures and other books had not come up with us. But it had been impossible, so near the coronation, to obtain the necessary porters. In November, however, the long expected books arrived; and during three days (Nov. 11-13) those of us who were living at Ambòdin' Andohàlo (where the old Girls' Central School now stands), were busy from morning till evening supplying the wants of the many applicants. During these three days we disposed of 922 Testaments and 515 portions (most of which were paid for), and several thousands of other books and tracts. The eagerness of the people and their radiant faces, as they became possessors of the precious volume they had so earnestly longed for, was a rich reward for all our trouble during these three busy days.

Soon after our arrival, Dr. Davidson began his medical work, and Mr. Parrett set up his press at Imarivolànitra. In these early days of course only reprints could be published, and the work of the first missionaries bore useful fruit. I do not think that any of their literary work perished during the persecution. The small catechisms that are now so widely used perhaps came nearer destruction than any other book. I do not remember having seen more than the two or three soiled and much worn copies obtained by us soon after our arrival. But these sufficed to provide copy for new editions, and from 1863 onwards, year after year these two useful summaries of Bible teaching have been circulated by thousands.

The brightness and hopefulness of our arrival was eight months after clouded over by the assassination of the king by whom we had been welcomed. But his successor Queen Rasohèrina confirmed the charter of religious freedom, and our work was not hindered.

The five years of Rasohèrina's reign (1863–1868) had an important bearing on the history of Christianity, and formed a season of quiet and patient ploughing and sowing that prepared the way for the great harvest of outward progress that took place on the accession of her successor.

Before Rasohèrina was proclaimed queen by the officers, she was required to sign a paper containing seven articles, one of which stated in the strongest possible terms that Christianity should never more be forbidden or hindered by the Government of Madagascar. Though the new queen was personally unfavourable to the Christian religion, she never, during the five years of her reign, deviated from this agreement, the acceptance of which was made a condition of her assuming the crown. Though no favour was shown to the Christians, and though they were often subjected to petty annoyances by those in power, and alarmed by rumours of a renewed outbreak of persecution, the work of our mission was allowed to go on without check or hindrance. The staff of missionaries was increased, and during this reign there were ten or eleven agents of the London Missionary Society engaged in the various branches of mission work. Preaching in town and country, guiding and aiding in the development of church life, instructing the many applicants for baptism and church membership, superintending and helping schools both on Sundays and week days, and above all, conducting Bible classes, which in those days formed a most important and fruitful branch of our work—these were the chief agencies employed by us to help and encourage the churches and to extend our work.

The missionaries were accustomed to hold their Bible classes on different days of the week, and many of the most earnest young men were in the habit of attending almost all of them. I remember a preacher in one of our united monthly prayer-meetings, when expatiating on the religious privileges of the people of Antananarivo, enumerating these classes, and telling the people they could go on Monday to such and such a class, on Tuesday to another, and so on through the days of the week, until he came to Saturday. For this day he could think of no particular religious teaching, but fell back on the general duty of cleanliness as a suitable preparation for Sunday, and called it, as it truly is in and around Antananarivo, 'Washing Day.'

Other branches of mission work were being gradually developed during this reign. Mr. Parrett was training his native printers, and preparing for the great demands which, all unknown to them, were soon to be made upon them. Dr. Davidson had built the first hospital at Anàlakèly, and was winning the people by his kindness and skill, and at the same time sapping the foundations of many of their old beliefs. Mr. Sibree had been engaged in erecting to the memory of the martyrs the Memorial Churches, which, in response to a happy inspiration of Mr. Ellis, the churches of England so generously gave to the churches of Madagascar.

We knew that the religion of the Lord Jesus Christ was winning its way, and that in the end it would be victorious. We did not, however, foresee how soon the downfall of the old idolatry would come. Seven years after the reopening of the mission the successor of Queen Rasohèrina, who bore the name of Ranavàlona II., became a Christian, and soon after she burnt the national idols. The people at once followed the example of their sovereign, and for some weeks the whole of Imèrina was given up to the novel task of idol

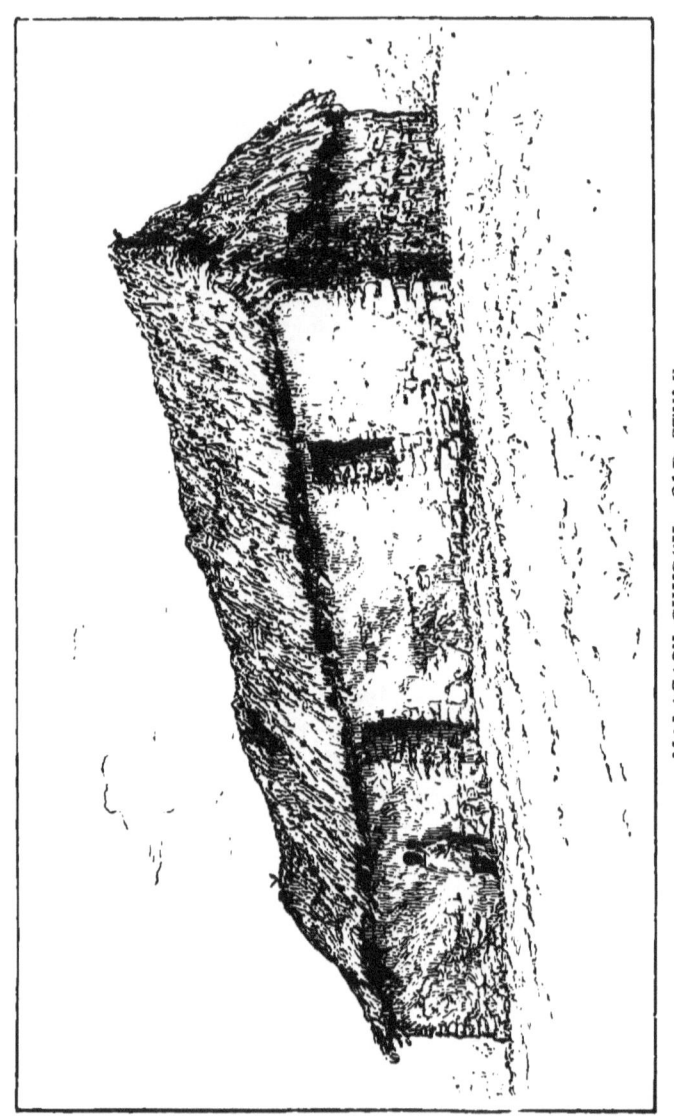

MALAGASY CHURCH—OLD STYLE.

burning. I have no space here to narrate in detail the course of subsequent events; but from a missionary standpoint the most important result of the profession of Christianity by the Queen and Prime Minister was that immense numbers of people came suddenly under Christian teaching. One single fact will be enough to make this point clear. In 1867 there were only ninety-two congregations (with 13,682 adherents) under the care of the London Missionary Society; three years later the number of congregations was 621 (with 231,759 adherents). This sudden accession of thousands of semi-heathen people, who, as the natives say, came rushing into the churches like a flock of sheep, has done much to lower the tone of Christian life; and no one can rightly understand the nature of the work now going on in Madagascar, or the many weaknesses of the native churches, or the difficulties that beset the missionaries, unless this fact be borne in mind.

Still, in looking upon the burning of the national idols, removed from us as it is by more than a quarter of a century, we see that it forms a great landmark in the history of Madagascar. It was a definite break with the past, a renunciation of the old worship, and a true step forward. And since that event much has been done, and much is still being done, to leaven with Christian truth these masses of half-instructed adherents. The story of the London Missionary Society, and of other societies at work in Madagascar, from 1869 onwards is simply the story of how they have been trying to instruct, help, and guide these tens of thousands of men and women who have embraced the religion of their sovereign, have built houses of prayer in their villages, and have placed thousands of children under instruction in the schools. There is in this story little to appeal to the imagination. There are no thrilling stories of adventure and danger to tell. The halo of romance that so often surrounds the earlier stages of mission work has long vanished, and at times the present work may seem dull and prosaic. But to those who estimate aright the value of abiding spiritual influences, this work of helping to guide and educate a young Christian community is one which must be full of interest, and must be acknowledged to possess undeniable claims to our sympathy and support.

CHAPTER X.

BIBLE TRANSLATION.

THE Christianity of our converts in Madagascar has been described by Romanists as consisting mainly in 'reading the Bible.' Happily there is some truth in this remark. The Bible has taken a deep hold on the minds of the people. Love of the Bible was one of the most marked characteristics of the persecuted Christians; and I see no prospect of the Bible losing its supreme place in the love and esteem of the people.

It will not be unfitting in this brief account of Madagascar, and how Christian work has been carried on among its people, to give here a short account of the care and labour undergone in order to provide for them a well-considered and faithful translation of the Scriptures. Missionaries may in time be no longer needed, but the Bible they brought to the knowledge of the people, and which formed the basis of all their teaching, will remain as a perennial source of instruction, and as a universally acknowledged standard.

The story of the Malagasy Bible is full of living interest, and it shows where among Protestant missionaries of all societies the one centre of union is to be found.

In sketching this story we must first of all go back in imagination to the middle of the seventeenth century, a time of great activity on the part of European nations, eager to found colonies in newly-discovered lands. Among other enterprises the French attempted to gain a footing at the south-east corner of Madagascar. The principal point occupied by them was Fort Dauphine, where, as we have already seen in Chapter VII., French missionaries settled, and began to instruct the natives in the Roman Catholic faith. This mission was maintained in spite of many discouragements and hardships for nearly twenty years. The missionaries, we are told, 'prepared catechisms, prayers, confessions to the Virgin Mary, and to St. Michael, and John the Baptist, with the command of the church to abstain from flesh on Fridays and Saturdays;' but we do not read that they translated even one of the Gospels.

This French mission, from causes we cannot now stop to consider, came to an end without leaving any permanent trace upon the natives; and the Protestant missionaries who a century and a half later carried the gospel to Madagascar, found it virgin soil. They went to a people without a written language, and without any knowledge of the Christian faith. Both in their literary and in their evangelistic labours they had not to revive a work that was dying out, but to start *de novo*, and seek in their own way to carry out the objects of their mission. To all who study the question, it is perfectly clear that the foundation of the work at present being carried on in Madagascar is not to be sought in the earlier attempts of the French missionaries in the south-east corner of the island, but in the work of the first missionaries of the London Missionary Society in and around Antananarivo, the capital.

Who, then, were these men to whom the Malagasy people owe their written language and their first translation of the Scriptures? They were, as we have seen, two Welshmen, both Davids— David Jones and David Griffiths. The first of these reached Antananarivo in 1820, the second a year later. The late Mr. Cameron describes Mr. Griffiths as a strong, hardy-looking man of middle height, accustomed to work and to overcome difficulties, a man quick in movement and of untiring energy. Mr. Jones, he also tells us, was tall and slightly built, much weakened by early attacks of the Tamatave fever, and easily tired. These two men were the pioneers of Protestant missions in Madagascar.

The main strength of these early missionaries was devoted to educational work, in which they were vigorously supported and encouraged by King Radàma I. and by Mr. Hastie, the British agent. But notwithstanding the many claims made upon them by this and other branches of work, they began very early to make a translation of the Scriptures. In this they were greatly assisted by some of their more promising scholars to whom they had taught the English language, and who in Madagascar are still spoken of as 'The Twelve;'[1] twelve young men having been selected by the

[1] The last of these men, Rainisoa Ratsimandisa, died in 1888.

missionaries for the more advanced positions. We cannot now stop to trace the growth of the translation; suffice it to say, that by March, 1830, ten years after the arrival of Mr. Jones in Antananarivo, a first edition of 3000 copies of the New Testament was completed. Thus within ten years after their arrival in Antananarivo, these pioneers of missionary work had not only mastered the early difficulties of learning the language and reducing it to writing, but had also given to the people this translation as the first fruits of their labours.

Even at this time much progress had been made in the translation of the Old Testament. In the completion and revision of this work valuable assistance was rendered by colleagues who had more recently joined the mission, viz. the Revs. D. Johns and J. J. Freeman.

The story of the completion of the printing of the Old Testament possesses peculiar interest. Soon after the death of King Radàma I., in 1828, the missionaries saw clear indications of the uncertainty of their position. Ominous clouds began to gather, until at length, in 1835, the storm of bitter persecution burst upon the infant church as narrated in a previous chapter. The edict of Queen Ranavàlòna I. against the Christian religion was published on March 1, 1835. At this time from Ezekiel to Malachi and a portion of Job remained unprinted. Thus, before the whole of the book was in the hands of the people, it was placed under a ban: an indubitable testimony to the power it had begun to exercise in the island. The wish of the missionaries to complete their work was only intensified by this outbreak of persecution. They toiled unremittingly, nothing daunted by the difficulties that beset them. The hostility of the government to Christianity was bitter and determined. The missionaries were almost deserted by their converts. They could procure no workmen to assist them in the printing. Mr. Baker, as the sheets of the translation were put into his hands, composed the whole himself; and Mr. Kitching worked off the sheets at the press. With trembling haste did the missionaries proceed with their task; and by the end of June they had the joy of seeing the first bound copies of the complete Bible.

Most of these Bibles were secretly distributed among the converts; and seventy remaining copies were buried for greater safety in the earth; precious seed over which God watched, and which in due time produced a glorious harvest. The translators were driven away; but the book they had translated remained. Studied in secret and at the risk of life, this first translation served during more than a quarter of a century of persecution to keep alive faith in the newly received religion. In the thrilling story of the Martyr Church one fact stands out with great clearness, viz. that as intense hatred of the Bible was shown by the persecuting queen and her counsellors, so was intense love of the Bible one of the most marked characteristics of the persecuted.

But this Bible has since been revised. Why, some will ask, did a translation so honoured of God need revision? The simple answer to this is that it was a first translation; and those who have studied the question of Bible translation are fully aware that in almost no instance has a first translation stood the test of time. Since 1830 great strides have been made in Biblical scholarship; and at the same time we may, without wishing in any way to slight the grand work of these first missionaries, safely assert that the Malagasy language is better understood now than it was in their days.

When, after the reopening of the mission in 1862, and especially after the great expansion of the work consequent upon the burning of the idols in 1869, missionaries began to look forward to the future, they felt that it was incumbent upon them to make some attempt to give to the Christians of Madagascar a more accurate and idiomatic version of the Scriptures. In 1872 a conference of missionaries, representing the five Protestant societies at that time working in Madagascar, was held in Antananarivo; and proposals for a revision were submitted to the British and Foreign Bible Society. This society generously accepted the whole pecuniary responsibility of the undertaking, and a Revision Committee was formed and began its work in the following year.

The present writer was, in accordance with the wish of his co-workers, appointed principal reviser and chairman of the Revision Committee. It was his duty to prepare a preliminary version as a basis for the committee's work, and also to act as editor and give practical effect to all the committee's decisions.

The committee consisted of eight foreigners (English, American, and Norwegian) and three natives. The first meeting was held on Dec. 1, 1873, and the work was completed on April 30, 1887. Many changes took place in the *personnel* of the committee during the progress of the revision, and only two Europeans and one native remained members from its foundation till its dissolution. Deducting interruptions, the time actually spent on the revision was about eleven years, of which nine and a half were spent on the first revision, and one and a half on the second and final revision.

During the greater part of the time, the committee met every Wednesday, and held morning and evening sittings of three hours each. Progress was at first but slow, sometimes not more than twelve verses being revised in a day; but the speed gradually improved, and the work averaged from sixty to eighty verses per day. The revision took a longer time than had been anticipated, and made large demands upon the patience of those engaged in it. But it had in it much that was pleasant and attractive, and served as a bond of union among missionaries of different communions. There were on the revision committee Anglicans, Lutherans, Presbyterians, Independents, and Friends; and the union of these in common work gave an easily appreciated answer to the taunt of the Jesuits, who delight to talk of 'the five different religions' introduced into Madagascar by Protestants. The natives see clearly that whatever divisions exist among these missionaries, all are at one in their loyalty to God's Word, and in their desire that the churches of Madagascar should possess as accurate and carefully considered a translation of it as modern scholarship renders possible.

From first to last native help was sought on all points of idiom and phraseology. A good Malagasy dictionary exists, one that has recently been greatly enlarged and improved by the Rev. J. Richardson, and a copy of this always lay on our table; but, as a matter of fact, it was but seldom opened, because seated at the bottom of the table was a living dictionary in the persons of our three native helpers. We felt increasingly the value of their help, and the second revision was in the main entrusted to them, working under the superintendence of the principal reviser. The whole Bible was once more read through with a view to the removal of anything harsh in style, and to make it as simple and harmonious as possible. If in future years it should be found that a version acceptable to the people generally has been produced, very much of the credit will be due to the patience and zeal of these native helpers.

Prayer and painstaking, we are told, will accomplish anything. In this revision work neither were spared. The labour of twelve years were given to it, and the best critical aids within the reach of the revisers were constantly used. Much prayer also was offered to Almighty God for the success and usefulness of the work. Every meeting was opened with prayer, and work thus begun and continued in prayer was suitably closed with a public thanksgiving service. This was held at the suggestion of the native brethren. The place of meeting was the stone memorial church at Ambònin' Ampamarìnana—the church built just on the edge of the precipice over which the fourteen Christians were hurled in the year 1849, because of their love to God's Word and their unwillingness to renounce the Saviour that Word had made known to them.

To this meeting the Queen of Madagascar sent His Excellency Rainilaiàrivòny, the Prime Minister, with a message of thanks to all who had taken part in the work. He told us in his speech of the deep interest that had been taken in this revision by the late queen, Ranavàlona II., the first Christian Sovereign of Madagascar, and how, taking that special interest in maintaining the purity of the language which is so often noticed in those of noble birth, she had often spoken of the revision to the natives engaged in it, and had occasionally herself suggested to them certain suitable expressions. He also told us that the present queen, Ranavàlona III., bid him say how thankful she was that a work that would tend so greatly to benefit her kingdom was at length completed.

What a lesson of patience and hope is this! From this very spot had Christians at the command of the first Queen Ranavàlona been hurled over the rocks because of their loyalty to God's Word; and thirty-eight years afterwards another Queen Ranavàlona took part, by her representative, in a service of rejoicing and thanksgiving that her people were soon to possess an improved translation of the Bible for which their fathers suffered so much. Truly God teaches us to wait patiently for Him.

All friends of Madagascar will re-echo the wish that this new translation may do much for the building up of the Christian community in that land. There are already more than 300,000 Protestant Christians there; and in some 2000 congregations and in nearly as many schools will this book be used. The past history of Madagascar has done much to awaken the sympathy of British Christians; let all then breathe a prayer that the future may be not unworthy of all that is noble and inspiring in the past; and that this new version of the Bible may be a potent factor in bringing about a result so devoutly to be desired.

CHAPTER XI.

THE PRESENT STATE OF CHRISTIANITY IN THE ISLAND.

WHAT then are the results of three-quarters of a century of Christian work in Madagascar? Has it become in any full sense of the term a Christian land?

That we may give in brief an answer to this question we will take in order the various missionary societies engaged in the work.

The London Missionary Society, as we have seen, began its work at Tamatave in the year 1818, and two years later the first missionary of the society arrived in Antananarivo. It was the first society in the field, and it had the honour of laying the foundation of the extensive work now being carried on, and as a consequence it holds a position second to no other society at work in the island. From the statistics for the year 1894 we find that it has 38 missionaries in Madagascar. These have under their care 1,328 congregations (about 800 of which are in Imèrina) with an aggregate of 280,000 adherents, 63,000 of whom are church members. It has nearly 1000 day schools containing 74,000 children. There are 1061 native pastors, very few of whom, however, are college-trained men, and

5879 preachers. The churches raise and use for local purposes £6000 or £7000 per annum.

The Church Missionary Society began a work on the east coast in 1864; but on the appointment of a bishop representing more particularly the High Church party in 1874 it removed its missionaries, and has not renewed its work.

The Society for the Propagation of the Gospel sent missionaries to Tamatave in 1864, and in 1872 began to work in the capital. In 1874 it sent out Bishop Kestell-Cornish, who still remains at the head of the Anglican mission, and has a large stone cathedral in the centre of the capital. The European agents of the society now number eight or ten, and the total number of congregations under their care is 27, with a total of about 10,000 adherents, 6000 (?) of whom are communicants. There are probably 2000 or 3000 scholars in the schools under the care of this society.

The Norwegian Missionary Society sent out two missionaries, Messrs. Engh and Nilsen, in the year 1866. Since that date its work has been greatly extended and developed, until it has now a larger number of missionaries than any other Protestant society. The last report gives the number of Norwegian missionaries as 44, with whom are associated 60 native ordained ministers, having charge of 50,000 or 60,000 adherents, 28,000 of whom are communicants. The number of children in the Norwegian schools is about 30,000.

The Society of Friends sent out to Madagascar in 1867 Mr. Joseph S. Sewell and Mr. and Mrs. Street. In the early years the work of the Friends was mainly educational, but it has gradually become more general, and now embraces all the ordinary departments of missionary work. Their mission is carried on in thorough harmony and friendly co-operation with the London Missionary Society, and they have given to all interested in Christian missions a splendid object lesson of unselfish service. No attempt has been made to detach congregations from the older society into whose labours they entered. The large country district under the care of the Friends is one of the most carefully worked in the country, and enjoys a fuller measure of English superintendence than the London Missionary Society has found it possible to give to its more widely extended operations. The educational work has been carefully developed and is deserving of the highest praise, while a well-managed printing office is always increasing the number of useful works available for general use. The Friends are also mainly responsible for the medical work to be noticed separately below. The present number of missionaries belonging to the Friends' Foreign Mission Association working in Madagascar is about 15. Under their care they have 149 congregations with 25,000 adherents and 2915 communicants. The Friends admittedly exercise a powerful influence, and do much to mould public opinion on all questions affecting the moral and spiritual well-being of the people.

Summarising the preceding paragraphs we may say that there are about 107 foreign Protestant missionaries in the island, having under their care

2004 congregations with a total of 375,000 adherents, more than 96,000 of whom are church members ; and that the Protestant schools contain 120,000 children.

To these we must add the statistics of the Roman Catholic mission. This comprises about 100,000 adherents, who are under the care of 113 foreign missionary agents. The children in the Roman Catholic schools are said to number 15,000.

We thus reach a total of more than 400,000 Christians ; and if we reckon the population of the island at 4,000,000 this will give one-tenth as the proportion of the Christian to the heathen population. It can never be too plainly or too frequently impressed upon the attention of the friends of missions that nine-tenths of the people of Madagascar remain heathen, and that of the remaining one-tenth who have accepted our religion many are Christians only in name.

It is nevertheless abundantly manifest that the Christian religion has taken a firm hold on the people. Perhaps the most noticeable indication of this is the number and prominence of the church buildings, especially in and around the capital. There are for instance the four stone Memorial Churches, built at the cost of the friends of the London Missionary Society to remind coming generations of the fidelity of the martyrs. Then some mention should be made of other church buildings, such, for example, as the large stone Cathedral of St. Lawrence, belonging to the Anglican mission, and the very fine and well-situated Roman Catholic cathedral in Ambòdin'

AMPATONAKÀNGA MEMORIAL CHURCH.

Andohàlo. From any of the higher points in Antananarivo may also be seen dozens of country churches, many of them well planned and well built structures. Even the poorer churches are a clear proof of the spread of the religion we have carried to Madagascar; and if we are at times disposed to think them mean and unsuited to their purpose, we must judge them not by our English standards, but by comparing them with the poor and comfortless dwellings in which most of the natives live.

Some few of the educational establishments are also 'outward and visible signs' of the elevating and enlightening work that is going on. The ordinary day-schools are carried on in the churches, but the higher education has required the erection of special buildings, belonging both to the Protestant and to the Roman Catholic Missions. Among these the large College of the London Missionary Society, standing on the top of the Faravòhitra Hill, is perhaps the building most likely to attract public attention. Here a work of much importance is being carried on. From the commencement of the college in 1869 to the present time some 300 or 400 young men have been educated in its classes. The majority of these have been theological students; but some have taken only the general non-theological subjects. The influence of the college has been widely felt, and men may be found in all parts of the country who have received their education within its walls. A large number even of the theological students become in time government officials. If one were to land to-day at one of the ports of Madagascar, he would probably see a gentleman with a cocked hat, and gold epaulettes and much gold lace upon his coat, with a band of music and a great number of soldiers and attendants following him. This would be the Governor, the representative of Queen Ranavàlona III. If this grand gentleman were visited privately he would probably begin to talk of the Rev. R. Toy or the Rev. G. Cousins, his former tutors in the London Missionary Society College.

The London Missionary Society College is not the only institution of this kind, similar establishments are carried on by the Society for the Propagation of the Gospel mission at Ambàtoharànana, and by the Norwegian Missionary Society at Fianarantsòa.

It must always be borne in mind that all educational work in Madagascar depends upon the aid and superintendence of the various missionary societies. There is a strong government influence in favour of education, but that is all. The only schools to which children can go are the mission schools, for no others exist.

Printing presses are another indication of the intellectual awakening that has taken place. Instead of the one small press taken out by us in 1862, there are now five well-equipped printing-offices at work in Antananarivo. Malagasy literature is still in its infancy, and a very few yards out of the thirty miles said to be required for the books in the British Museum would accommodate all the books at present existing in

THE LONDON MISSIONARY SOCIETY'S COLLEGE.

the language. Still the foundations are being laid and progress is being made both as to the number and quality of the books published.

All medical work and the training of young men as native doctors is another direct fruit of missionary work. Dr. Davidson, as we have seen, was the honoured pioneer in this department of work, and his name is still remembered and loved by many of his old friends. The hospital he built at Anàlakèly did excellent service ; but at length it was found necessary to seek a more open and healthy site, and the present building at Isoàvinandrìana, about a mile away from the capital, was erected. Here a most valuable work is carried on. Hospital and dispensary work, the training of native nurses, and the education of medical students, are alike cared for. An air of order and quiet, of cheerfulness and brightness, reigns at Isoàvinandrìana ; and all residents in and around the capital highly appreciate the advantage of having so well-managed a hospital within an easy distance. The nurses trained by Miss Byam are highly valued, and they deserve all the praise bestowed upon them. The medical students at the close of their course are subjected to examinations arranged by a medical board comprising all the Protestant doctors. Successful students receive the diploma of M.M.M.A. (Member of the Madagascar Medical Association).

The Norwegian Society has also a large hospital in the capital under the care of Dr. Thèsen ; and the government also employs a doctor, who carries on some dispensary work. The Roman Catholic priests and the Sisters of Mercy have always been active in attending to the sick ; and of late years the French government, copying the methods of the missionary societies, has established free dispensaries as a means of winning the good will of the natives.

Work among the lepers, a class which, alas! is to be found in all parts of Madagascar, has long been carried on by the French missionaries. There is also an important leper settlement at Antsirabè, in the Betsilèo country under the care of the Norwegian Society ; and the Rev. P. G. Peake, of the London Missionary Society, has begun a similar work near his station at Isoàvina.

As a result of all this work which missionaries of different societies are doing, there is undoubtedly a great intellectual, moral, and social movement observable among the people, at least, in the main centres such as Antananarivo and Fianàrantsòa. The inhabitants of these districts are, speaking generally, Christian people. Any one visiting these places on a Sunday would see what crowds attend to various religious services ; and the quiet and order that reign in them on the Sunday has often been remarked by strangers.

Nor are church-going and Sunday observance the only signs of change. Those who know well the life of the people are able to testify as to the gradual advance that is being made. A new standard of morality has been introduced, and absolutely new ideas as to marriage, home life, and the care of children, are beginning to exert their influence. Polygamy has nearly disappeared, and

THE NEW HOSPITAL AT ISOÀVINANDRIÀNA.

divorce can only be obtained after a proper trial before the judges. Home life is becoming purified, and a generation of young people is growing up who have received from childhood a Christian education, and have been shielded to some extent from the prevailing corruption.

A purifying leaven is working and will work; but the old habits and customs of heathenism are not easy to destroy, and we often have to grieve over their recrudescence, and have to acknowledge that superstition dies hard.

Much is done by preaching and by the press to create a healthy public opinion on all moral questions. Much, too, is done by united meetings of the churches to secure oneness of purpose and harmony of sentiment on all questions affecting their well-being.

As a healthy sign of growth may be named the tendency of the younger Christians to form societies, such, for instance, as a Bible society, a tract society, a preachers' society, an orphanage society. Much good work is carried on by these societies, and an aggressive spirit is growing. The native missionary society sends its agents to far-off tribes, and is just now endeavouring to increase its useful work. Young people's societies of Christian Endeavour are being formed in many places, and the young Christians banded together in this way do much to help one another, and to extend the influence of the Gospel.

This chapter would not be complete without a few words about the work of the Roman Catholic missionaries. As a Protestant missionary I have, of course, no knowledge of the inner working of their mission ; but no one can live long in Madagascar without learning to admire the self-denial and patience with which their work is carried on. The educational work in Tamatave and in Antananarivo is specially deserving of high commendation.

Rather than attempt myself to summarise the work of the Roman Catholic missionaries, I will transcribe part of an account written a few years since by an English visitor :—

'In 1861, when Catholic missionaries landed on the shores of Tamatave, there was not a Catholic in the island ; but little by little, by dint of unwearied labours, sufferings and preachings, they won over, not hundreds, but thousands of pagans to the knowledge and love of our Lord and His truth, so that their pagan converts number now over 130,000.

'They have built a magnificent cathedral which is the glory and pride of Tananarivo. They have also 300 churches and 414 Catholic stations scattered over this island. Connected with these churches they have innumerable schools, where 18,000 children are taught and trained by a large and devoted staff of Christian brothers, of sisters of St. Joseph of Cluny, and 641 native teachers.

'They have also created industrial schools, where various trades are taught by two devoted brothers, Benjamin and Arnaud ; and at Ambòhipò they have a flourishing college for young Malgaches, They have also in the island four large dispensaries, where thousands of prescriptions are distributed

gratis to all who seek relief in their sufferings. They have also established a leper hospital at Ambàhivòraka, where the temporal and spiritual wants of 150 poor lepers are freely administered to; and they are about to open another such establishment in Betsileo-land.

'The wretched prisons of the city are also looked after by the zealous Father Baryt, who, like a second St. Peter Claver, weekly dispenses gratis rice, clothing, chains (?) too, and spiritual instruction and consolation to the half-starved, half-naked prisoners, for the government does nothing more for them than find them a miserable shelter! A most touching sight it is to see him among these poor skeleton-looking creatures administering to their wants.

'Their literary labours are also worth mentioning. In Tananarivo they have a large printing house superintended by Father Malzac. Their catalogue of books shows the numberless devotional, literary, and scientific works that they have edited and published in the Malgache language. Father Malzac is now occupied in bringing out a dictionary in Malgache.

'They have built also on the hill of Ambohidempona, facing the capital, a magnificent observatory, which is the most imposing structure that the eye of the traveller sees as he approaches from Tamatave, the great Hova city......

'All are familiar also with the famous map of Madagascar, drawn up with so much care and skill by Père Roblet.

'The name of Father Combonè, the naturalist,

is not unknown to the European and American literary world, to whose reviews he often contributes scientific articles on matters relating to this wonderful island. . . .

'Such are some of the heroic works of evangelisation and civilisation which the present missionaries are carrying on in that far-off island continent in the Indian seas.'

I have allowed the work of the Roman Catholic missionaries to be described by the pen of a friendly visitor. To much in the Roman Catholic system we may be strenuously opposed; to their zeal and skill, their self-denial and their patience, we render the homage of our ungrudging admiration.

I would also add here that happily we have not at present in Madagascar had to complain of any deep bitterness between Roman Catholics and Protestants. We have no Orange riots to trouble us. Even Frenchmen allow that the London Missionary Society has been true to its belief in religious toleration.

Père Causseque, a well-known member of the Jesuit mission, has said : 'There are English and Norwegian missions at Antananarivo, and if their relations are not intimate with the Catholic missions, they are civil. The English and Norwegians do not attack the Catholics. The open and violent enemies of the latter are French.'

The fullest religious liberty is enjoyed in Madagascar to-day, and I do not think there is any prospect of either French or English missionaries enjoying under a French protectorate a fuller measure of freedom of action than that enjoyed by all classes under the present *régime*. A letter published recently in the *Times* newspaper, written by Father Vaughan, seems to show that this is the judgment of the Roman Catholics themselves, and that they do not anticipate with much pleasure the prospect of coming under French rule.

But it should also be borne in mind that French influence in Tahiti and other South Sea Islands has been adverse both to morality and to Evangelical Christianity, and all friends of Christian Missions in Madagascar cannot help looking with serious misgivings to a future in which French influence may become predominant.

CHAPTER XII.

THE POLITICAL SITUATION.

ONCE more the name of Madagascar is to be seen day by day in our newspapers, and we are beginning to wonder what will be the next step of the French Government, and what will be the attitude of the Hova.

From questions addressed to me since my return from Madagascar, I know that many are anxious to understand the exact position of affairs at this present time, and to know what have been the causes that have led up to the present crisis. An attempt will be made in the present chapter to meet this wish.

The events of the next few months may be of vast importance in the history of Madagascar, and may have great influence for good or for evil on the future development of Christianity among the people.

The explanation of the present lies in the past, and we are able with more or less correctness to explain how things have come to be as they are, if we can trace out the preceding steps in their development.

The story of France and Madagascar is now a very old one. In the seventeenth century the

French occupied Fort Dauphine, at the south-east extremity of the island, and also formed establishments at Foule Point and other places on the east coast. The lives of many Frenchmen were sacrificed in the attempt to maintain these positions, and finally they were all but abandoned. In the Napoleonic wars, when Great Britain seized Mauritius and Bourbon, she also acquired whatever possessions and rights France possessed in Madagascar. And although, when peace was re-established after the battle of Waterloo, Bourbon was restored to France, all French rights and possessions in Madagascar were retained by Great Britain. Later on, in the time of Radàma I. (1810–1828), when a treaty of friendship was entered into between him and Governor Farquhar in 1817, all these claims were finally renounced, and Radàma was acknowledged King of Madagascar. The French, however, never altogether abandoned the idea that Madagascar in some sense belonged to them. A work was published in 1859 entitled *Madagascar; a French Possession from the year* 1642, showing how there still lingered in the minds of many the idea that, as a result of these early establishments, France still possessed some claims on the island.

Later on France acquired by treaty with local chiefs the islands of St. Mary (1821), near the eastern coast, and Nosibè (1841) on the north-west.

In 1845, owing to a decree of Queen Ranavàlona I., requiring all foreign traders in Tamatave either to submit absolutely to Malagasy law and custom or at once to leave Madagascar, an attack was made upon the Hova fort in Tamatave by several French and English vessels of war. It was found impossible to take the fort without proper breaching artillery, and the storming party retired, leaving behind them the bodies of several who had been killed during the attack. The heads of these men were stuck on poles near the beach, where they remained for some years. The Malagasy always claim this as a victory ; but from an account published by an eye-witness, it seems that, while the French and English lost only twenty-one killed and fifty-six wounded (including one English and three French officers), the Hova loss was very great —a runaway estimated it at 400. Still the fact remains that the fort was not taken.

For many years the Malagasy have lived in constant dread of a French invasion. Mr. Ellis, on his visit to the island in 1856, found reports of such a threatened invasion a source of alarm and unsettlement. And from the accession of Radàma II. there have been constant difficulties between the French and Malagasy governments. The repudiation of the Lambert treaty was one cause of trouble, and this cost the Malagasy £48,000 by way of indemnity. In the year 1868 a treaty of friendship was entered into by the two governments, and Queen Rasohèrina was recognised as Queen of Madagascar. This seemed to be the final abandonment of all French claims. It did not, however, end the difficulties. Other causes of complaint arose, and another indemnity was paid.

In 1883, because the Malagasy would not yield to certain demands made by the French, war broke out. Without any warning the forts on the northwest were bombarded, and Mojangà was occupied. Soon after, Tamatave was taken, or rather, was abandoned by the Hova and occupied by the French. A fortified camp at Manjakandrianombàna, a few miles to the west of Tamatave, was formed by the Hova troops; and though Tamatave was held by the French for three years, and the camp at Manjakandrianombàna was within reach of their guns, and was constantly shelled by them, and several attempts were made to attack it, notably one which is known as the battle of Sahamàfy, the Hova still held their position till the end of the war.

In 1886 a treaty of peace was concluded, which, while reserving to the Hova the control of all domestic affairs, gave to the French a privileged position in regard to foreign affairs, and put all Malagasy living abroad under the protection of the French Government. A French residency was established in Antananarivo, where a resident-general resided, together with his staff and a guard of honour consisting of about fifty French soldiers. The large bay of Diego Suarez, on the north-east of Madagascar (sometimes known as British Sound) was also ceded to France.

This treaty was seen at the time to contain ambiguous phrases capable of very different interpretations, and as a matter of fact the French authorities and the Hova prime minister have never agreed as to its meaning, and much controversy and diplomatic discussion has arisen during the last eight years as to the exact extent of French rights in Madagascar. The word 'protectorate' was carefully excluded from the treaty; and it is well known that the Hova would not have signed it at all, if they had understood it to establish a French protectorate. There has been much friction and prolonged discussion on this point. But though the word was carefully excluded, the thing itself was in some form at least included. The thin end of the wedge was inserted, and the French trusted to the development of events and to the efforts of their successive residents-general to drive it home. So high an authority as M. le Myre de Vilers, however, clearly acknowledged in 1892 the limitations of the present so called protectorate. 'There are,' he said, 'several kinds of protectorates. Now the Hova never did accept or recognise the protectorate of France, as it is understood here (*i.e.* in France). When Admiral Miot and M. Patrimonio negotiated the treaty of peace, the prime minister sent them back the first draft which contained the word protectorate, asking that this word be erased, and adding that if it was maintained, the war would be resumed.'

Two points should be specially emphasised in our statement as to the difficulties that have arisen since 1886. The first is that together with the treaty there was an annex or explanatory document, signed by the French plenipotentiaries, M. Patrimonio and Admiral Miot, and it is perfectly certain that it was only on the ground of the explanations and limitations contained in this document that the treaty was agreed to by the Malagasy premier. This annex was suppressed when the treaty was brought before the French

Chambers, and has always been treated by French officials as so much waste paper. Much of the present difficulty has arisen from the ignoring of this document and the refusal to abide by its limitations.

Another burning question during the past eight years has been that of the *exequaturs* of the foreign consuls. The French claim that the consuls placed in Madagascar by the British, German, and American governments should receive their *exequaturs* through the French resident-general. To this claim the prime minister has never consented. In 1887 M. le Myre de Vilers hauled down his flag and left the capital, because the Hova would not consent to this claim. After a few days, however, he returned to the residency and yielded the point in dispute. But succeeding residents-general, returned to the old claim, and there has now been for some years a complete deadlock, as the prime minister has persistently refused to acknowledge any communications from the representatives of other powers which have reached him through the French resident-general.

Those familiar with Madagascar affairs have seen for some time that a crisis could not be long deferred. France was bound to do either more or less, or she would become the laughing-stock of Europe. She was claiming in the eyes of all the world to exercise a protectorate over Madagascar, whilst all the time her representatives were being baffled and thwarted by the astuteness of the prime minister, and they had hardly advanced their position a single step since the conclusion of the treaty in 1886. One after another the French residents-general have left Madagascar in disgust. They have learned by experience, what a well-known British official prophesied they would in time find out, viz., the immense power of passive resistance that exists in the Malagasy nature. Whilst outwardly treating the French officials with suavity and respect, the prime minister has managed, whether wisely or unwisely may be a matter of opinion, to outwit and disappoint all those who have hitherto had to enter into diplomatic relations with him. To watch the diplomatic struggle has been like watching two cautious and skilful players at chess. But the game has now reached a critical position, and in a few months we shall probably see who is in the end to be victorious.

The present action of the French is from their point of view inevitable. The *amour propre* of the French nation would be sorely wounded, if the idea of a protectorate had now to be finally renounced, and all recent action on their part seems to point to a determination to put forth a strenuous effort to make the French claims a reality, and to attain what has so long been the dream of the French nation, viz., a substantial foothold in Madagascar, and the power to control its government and the development of its immense material resources.

To Englishmen this may be a disappointment. There are friends of Madagascar who would heartily rejoice in the establishment of a British protectorate. It may be our national vanity that leads us to believe that we could so govern Madagascar as to benefit greatly the people themselves and to aid them in their upward progress ; but there are facts as to British influence in other parts of the world that seem to warrant such a belief.

The time has passed, however, for such a possibility. The Malagasy have missed their opportunity, and the hands of our own government are tied by their past action. It is believed by many that when Admiral Gore Jones was sent out as special ambassador in 1881 he was instructed to feel the pulse of the Malagasy government and to find out whether any wish for a British protectorate existed. Whether this is a correct surmise or not is known only to those who are in the confidence of the Foreign Office ; but it is an undoubted fact that neither in 1881 nor at any other date has there existed on the part of the ruling classes in Madagascar any wish to obtain British guidance and protection. There has always existed among the people generally, but especially among the higher classes, an intense desire to maintain their national independence.

The opinion is not uncommon that without some help from a nation of larger experience and wider knowledge, the Hova government will not be able to do for Madagascar all that is required for its firm and just government and for the development of its resources. A liberal and wise employment of European administrators and instructors with adequate power to control their own special departments might perhaps have met the requirements of the case and have averted the present difficulty. But the national jealousy and distrust of foreigners has made this impossible. Few

Europeans have been so employed, and those few have been so fettered in their action that they have never had a fair opportunity of doing their best to make their control as effective and beneficial as it might have been. It is not in the nature of the Hova so to trust a foreigner as to give him any large amount of freedom and authority.

Advice on this and other matters has been repeatedly given to the prime minister by travellers and others. The late well-known Mr. Cameron, special correspondent of the *Standard*, had a very free and earnest talk with him, and others have done the same. The advice has been, however, to a very large extent unheeded.

The English government will not oppose the French in their attempts to make good the position they claim in Madagascar. Somewhat prematurely, as it seemed to many, on August 5, 1890, Lord Salisbury acknowledged the French protectorate with all its consequences. The English have taken but a languid interest in Madagascar affairs, or such a cool giving away of a people who had always regarded us as their friends would have been impossible. It is true that a carefully-worded clause in the agreement runs, " In Madagascar the missionaries of both countries shall enjoy complete protection. Religious toleration and liberty for all forms of worship and religious teaching shall be guaranteed." This seems sufficiently definite, but the experience of Tahiti and Mare seems to indicate that after events should be very carefully watched.

The die is now cast, and sighs and regrets are useless. We shall watch with interest the mode in which the French will attempt to make good their position. Undoubtedly they have a very difficult work before them. They have to penetrate to the centre of Madagascar. There are no roads in our sense of the term. The country is very mountainous, and there are dense forests. Above all, malarial fever prevails throughout all the lower part of the country. At present when the French soldiers belonging to the resident-general's guard of honour are sent out, they are carried in palanquins like other travellers. An army cannot be so conveyed, but must push its way through marsh and forest and up the steep mountain tracks. Probably one-third of the soldiers would be *hors de combat* before reaching Antananarivo. This will all have to be allowed for in estimating the number of men required. To this must be added the difficulty of transport in a country where all things are carried on men's shoulders. Then a long line of communication of 200 or 300 miles will have to be defended from the harassing attacks of the Hova soldiers. Of these there are many thousands who have been well drilled and who are provided with European arms, including machine guns. Gunpowder has long been manufactured in the country, and recently a cartridge factory under the superintendence of two Englishmen has been started by the government. There is little doubt that a stubborn resistance will be offered to the French advance. But no one, I suppose, doubts that if France is really in earnest and is willing to sacrifice millions of francs and thousands of men to gain what may prove to be to her a source of weakness rather than of strength, she may before many months are over succeed in placing the French tricolour on the top of the great palace of Manjakamiàdana.

The difficulties of the French will not be ended by a victory in or near Antananarivo, and no victory on the coast would settle the question. After the power of the Hova is broken will come the problem how, without incurring an immense expenditure, France is to govern a country as large as or larger than her own against the will of the people. Had the goodwill of the Hova been gained, and had there been a willingness to accept a protectorate, the task would have been an easy one ; but the protectorate is being forced upon an unwilling people, and the war is likely to leave a legacy of hate and distrust that will not make the task of the French Government an easy one.

Granting the possibility, perhaps we should say, the probability, that the French will succeed in making the protectorate effective, how will this affect Protestant missions and the cause of Protestant Christianity generally ? Will the work of British and Norwegian missionaries be seriously hindered ?

To some this may seem but a secondary question, and they would rather ask : How will the wellbeing of the common people of Madagascar be affected by the event ? Will they, for instance, enjoy less or more freedom and security than they enjoy at the present ? Will they be less or more subject to oppression and unjust exaction from their superiors ? With regard to both enquiries the only possible answer at present seems to be, Time will show.

We may be sure that one of the first results

of French predominance in Madagascar would be the speedy opening up of the country by the construction of roads and railways, and by the development of its vast material resources. The cultivation of sugar, tea, coffee, vanilla, and other products would soon be carried on in a far more extensive and enterprising manner than at present. Scientific gold mining would also be developed rapidly. Three or four years ago the consular estimate was that over £110,000 worth of gold was obtained 'as a result of twelve months' scratching at the surface of the country's mineral deposits;' and I am informed on good authority that this estimate is far too low to represent the present state of the trade.

Speaking generally, we are, I think, justified in holding as possible that French administrators may govern with a broader view of the needs of the country, and with a deeper desire to rule justly and for the good of the whole community than seems possible to the present Hova rulers. These larger and juster ideas as to the functions of rulers are with European nations the result of long experience in the past; and it is perhaps not to be wondered at if the Prime Minister of Madagascar, and those under his control, should too often show how they lack this broad sense of justice and this steady and determined purpose of seeking to make their rule a blessing to the common people of the land. Government too often in their eyes becomes, what, indeed, it has not unfrequently been in lands boasting of a higher degree of civilisation than Madagascar, the means of enriching and exalting the few at the expense of the many. Still the record of France is not one that leads any close observer to feel at all sanguine as to the future. What she gives with one hand may very easily be more than taken away with the other. In the meantime it may well be hoped that the agreement of 1890 may furnish a sound working basis for any new system.

I think we have also some solid ground for hoping that we should still enjoy in Madagascar that priceless blessing that has now been the possession of the churches there for thirty years—I mean complete religious liberty. Omitting other weighty considerations, it appears reasonable to suppose that French statesmen will see how impolitic it would be to persecute 300,000 of the most intelligent and progressive people in the island. They will have difficulties in abundance before them in the great task they have undertaken, and will not care to add to those difficulties by a policy of intolerance and persecution.

We must remember, too, that Protestant missions in Madagascar are not exclusively in the hands of English missionaries. The Norwegians have a strong mission; and it seems reasonable to believe that if Madagascar should come more completely under French control, the Protestant churches of France would bestir themselves and come to the aid of their co-religionists in that island.

In concluding this chapter, let me say that I have the strongest conviction that the Protestant Christians in Madagascar will stand true and firm in their hour of trial. They are not a fickle people. They have been tested by the trials of the past, and I am sure they will not be lightly turned away from the faith they have accepted.

As Christians we must pray for peace and do our utmost to secure it. War is a terrible scourge. But we cannot read the history of the past without seeing how God has overruled this scourge of war to bring men to a more humble spirit, to teach them great lessons as to His government, and so to prepare them for a higher and better national life.

THE END.

LONDON:
PRINTED BY WILLIAM CLOWES AND SONS, LIMITED,
STAMFORD STREET AND CHARING CROSS.

www.ingramcontent.com/pod-product-compliance
Lightning Source LLC
Chambersburg PA
CBHW030309170426
43202CB00009B/938